THE STORY OF THE MARY ROSE

ERNLE BRADFORD

The Story of the
Mary Rose

W. W. Norton & Company
New York · London

Contents

O lord, methought what pain it was to drown,
What dreadful noise of waters in mine ears,
What sights of ugly death within mine eyes!
Methought I saw a thousand fearful wrecks;
A thousand men that fishes gnawed upon,
Wedges of gold, great anchors, heaps of pearl,
Inestimable stones, unvalued jewels,
All scattered in the bottom of the sea!

(William Shakespeare, Richard III, I.IV.)

Author's Introduction

The *Mary Rose*, flagship of King Henry VIII's Vice Admiral, Sir George Carew, sank off Portsmouth on Sunday July 19, 1545. Bound for action against an invading French Armada, she went down at Spithead with great loss of life, probably without having fired a shot. Now, in 1982, she is to be raised from the sea bed with the aid of the most skilful underwater archaeology and sophisticated modern technology.

For 437 years the flower of King Henry VIII's fleet, probably named after his sister Mary Tudor, has lain encapsulated by the silts of the Solent. Like the lava which held Pompeii frozen in time, these silts have preserved a whole Tudor world just as it was on that summer day when the *Mary Rose* sailed out to give battle.

I have attempted to tell something of the history of this great ship, of how she looked, and how she was fought and sailed. I am a writer, not an archaeologist, and any errors of fact or emphasis are my own. Every day as I was writing new discoveries were being made, and facts and figures were constantly having to be changed. This was literally history in the making, and I had long been used to writing about history that was established and, therefore, static. It is important to emphasise, then, that there will be assumptions or statements made in my account which time and the labour of experts will alter or more fully elucidate.

In 1981, for instance, a book was discovered in a box, about which little can be said at the time of writing though, under careful treatment and study, it may yet reveal something of its content. I saw an iron cannon shortly after it had been lifted. A large, grey corrugated tube dripping with silt and slime, it gave no indication – except to the trained eye – of the marvel of the gunfounder's craft that lay within. If I had not been staying in Portsmouth for some time, and then returning a few weeks later, I would have had no conception of what that particular "find" meant – nor what in due course it would mean to thousands of visitors to the *Mary Rose* museum in the years to come. When I saw it on the second occasion I was amazed by the change that had taken place and by the contrast between its known sixteenth century origins and its apparent gleaming newness. So skilfully had the archaeologists and the experts in conservation treated the gun that the sheen of dark iron must have been much the same as when the gunners of the *Mary Rose* bent over it four hundred years ago.

I was shown the sea-wasted cannon ball that had been loaded against the invader, the wad that lay between ball and charge, and even a heap of the granulated black powder that, at a touch from the linstock, would have fired it. I had seen history being recovered and now, thanks to the skills of many dedicated people, I saw history transformed into something immediately comprehensible. No book, however well written and researched, could do as much to restore a vanished age.

The excitement that pervaded the operations of raising the treasures of the *Mary Rose* and preparing to lift the hull was something that immediately communicated itself to me. Between the divers and the archaeologists and those who photographed, studied and conserved the newly found objects – whether guns, arrows, bows, domestic gear or knife hilts – there ran a current of enthusiasm that was instantly infectious. Everywhere I went I found the same atmosphere: it was as if a charge that had been fired in 1545 had reverberated in the late twentieth century, bringing to a whole new generation of Britons something of the sparkle and spring-time freshness of Tudor England.

Under the presidency of His Royal Highness, The Prince of Wales, the Mary Rose Trust has achieved a magnificent and impressive record of finds which sheds new light on the world of the Tudor mariner. In 1981 alone, over 7,000 artefacts were recovered, while nearly 1,500 structural timbers were removed to facilitate the transportation of the hull to the shore later in this year. A specially designed lifting frame will be used to bring King Henry VIII's great warship up from the sea bed. Like countless others I wait with mounting excitement for that day, this year, when she returns to her birthplace, Portsmouth.

Ernle Bradford
May, 1982

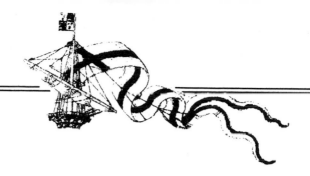

1. The French Invasion

It was July 18 and a French invasion fleet was in the Channel. Under the command of the Admiral of France, Monsieur d'Annebault, it began entering the Solent. King Henry VIII had come down south with the Privy Council on July 15 to prepare for the French attack and their possible landing, and to inspect the new fortifications he had recently built. He was dining with Viscount Lisle, High Admiral of England, in his flagship, *Henry Grace à Dieu*, when it was reported that the French ships had been sighted. They were strung out and rounding the Isle of Wight. The king gave his instructions to the fleet and hurried ashore to take charge and to rally the militia, while his admiral led out the English ships from Portsmouth harbour.

The time was when Henry would have been the first into the fray himself. Indeed, only the year previously he had led his troops over to Calais and had ridden a great charger to the siege of Boulogne. The horse must have been massive, for Henry by this time in his life was a man of enormous girth, as can be seen not only in portraits but from his last suit of armour (now in the Tower of London) where the armourer, working as carefully as any tailor, has allowed for the king's huge paunch. He had to be carefully hoisted on to his horse and, indeed, when indoors nowadays he was carried about in a chair and hauled upstairs by machinery. Eating and drinking an immense

The scene at Spithead, July 19 1545. Right (detail 1): The English fleet sails from Portsmouth to engage the enemy. Left (detail 2): The French fleet. Top centre (detail 3): French galleys engage the Henry Grace à Dieu. Centre (detail 4): The masts of the sunken Mary Rose. Bottom centre (detail 5): Henry VIII enters Southsea Castle. This eighteenth century engraving was based on a Tudor wall painting, now lost, that once belonged to Cowdray House in Sussex.

amount – perhaps, except for riding, his last delight in life – had transformed the king who had once been the flower of his age into a gross and badly-ageing figure. Furthermore, he had been ill off and on ever since 1528 when an ulcer had developed on one leg. In the summer of 1537 both legs had become infected and Henry had had to postpone a promised visit to the north, explaining privately to the Duke of Norfolk it was because of ''a humour which has fallen upon our legs''. It has sometimes been conjectured that the king had syphilis (common enough at the time) but there is no evidence for this, nor for him having received the well-established treatment for the disease. There were none of the other signs either in him or his children, and it is more probable that he developed varicose ulcers which would have been exacerbated by his constant activity.

As he rode towards Southsea Castle on that July day to watch his fleet come

Two details from the Cowdray engraving:
Left: Henry VIII, mounted on horseback, enters Southsea Castle.
Right: the English fleet, led by Henry's warship, the Henry Grace à Dieu *about to engage the French fleet in Spithead.*
Overleaf: The Henry Grace à Dieu *as depicted in the Antony Roll, an illustrated inventory of King Henry VIII's ships completed in 1546*

out and give battle to the French he was not in armour, but in the full Renaissance finery in which he had always delighted to dress. Although at fifty-four the king was a very far remove from the young monarch whom a dazzled Venetian had once described as "the handsomest potentate I ever set eyes on", he was still very much a king. Although ailing, he was still "the bluff king Hal" of legend, exulting in his power and glory. "His fingers were one mass of rings," wrote one Venetian ambassador, "and around his neck he wore a gold collar from which hung a diamond as big as a walnut." It is possible that on that July day in 1545 he wore round his neck the huge gold whistle encrusted with gemstones which he had worn on the occasion of the launching of the *Henry Grace à Dieu*, when he had first dined aboard her in October 1515. Southsea Castle towards which he now rode was one of his many creations. In 1539, when there had been another invasion scare, he had

begun a line of fortresses that ran from the Thames estuary through Sandgate, Deal, Walmer and Dover to the Isle of Wight.

The fleet which he awaited to emerge and engage the French was also very largely another of Henry's creations. He had inherited from his father a number of warships, but Henry had greatly enlarged the fleet. Portsmouth was very active throughout the years of his reign as he began a big ship-building programme. His father had largely kept clear of foreign entanglements, but Henry's pattern of kingship was very different indeed. When he had come to the throne he had had two basic options open to him: either to continue in the manner of his father, a civilian king engaged in law-enforcement and seeing to the financial state of his kingdom, or to return to the European concept of the martial monarch and to establish England as a European power. Henry chose the latter and, to the disadvantage of England's citizens and economy, once more involved his country in the endless tangle of European politics and petty wars. The so-called Hundred Years War was resumed.

Although Henry is often thought of as a Renaissance king, he was in fact backward-looking. The fleet which he had built up over the years was designed for the essentially negative aspect of dealing with continental neighbours – France in particular. It is true that, by lavishing large sums of

13

ffor Warre· ffor the

The Harry Tunayef= th: Grace a Dieu

Gonnes· of Brasse· Gonnes· of yron· Gonnepowder·

of. pro.... Shosse. of. Stoen   Bowes Bowestrynge..
          and leade   Arrowes Morrys pyki
                               Byllys Dartt for toppys

....ns C for Cannon peze lx   Bowes of yewgh vc   pikhamm
nous lx for porte pecys ccc   Bowestryng   Sledgys o
                                 Lyvere Arrowes   bnel   Crowes o

money on shipbuilding and dockyards such as Portsmouth and Deptford, he had laid the foundations of what would one day be England's triumphant navy. On the other hand, by concentrating his gaze upon Europe, Henry failed to look westward where the New World was opening up. From the Iberian peninsula the ships of Portugal and Spain were already engaged in laying the foundations of overseas empire and home prosperity. It was not

A famous picture of King Henry VIII embarking at Dover for France. The ship in the middle foreground is commonly supposed to be the Henry Grace à Dieu.

until the reign of Elizabeth I that her seamen would really begin to strike out westward only to find themselves largely forestalled – and it would be generations before England could rival the Portuguese and Spanish achievements.

Nevertheless, Henry's interest in, and enthusiasm for, continental wars inspired the development of the navy; for, of course, unlike the continentals

17

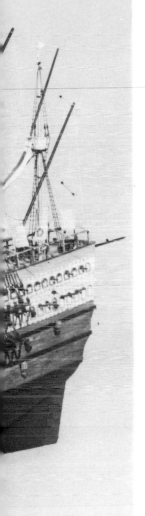

themselves, he could not engage in this stimulus without ships to transport
his troops and without warships to protect them. The ship aboard which he
had just been dining was an example of the new type of warship which was
just evolving and which, unchanged in essence, would dominate the seas of
the world for over three hundred years. The *Great Harry* (the *Henry Grace à
Dieu*) was a four-master of about 1,000 tons with massive castles rising fore
and aft from the waist. She could set a large press of sail, which would have
been much needed to shift her heavy hull; having both topmasts and
topgallant masts on her three forward masts, though on the bonaventure
(mizzen) above the aftercastle she had a topmast only. She was the third of her
name.

Built between 1512 and 1514, probably by Robert Bryandine, the
Clerk of the Ships, with William Bond, the naval architect, supervising, she
had originally been intended for a complement of 400 sailors, 260 soldiers,
and 40 gunners. The discrepancy between the number of soldiers and of
gunners shows that she was still a ship built to the medieval thinking of
"land warfare" at sea. This is reinforced by the fact that not only were 2,000
bows to be provided for her but thousands of arrows and bowstrings – and
even 200 suits of armour.

But the ship which Henry had just left had been radically altered since

those days. She had originally been clinker built after the fashion of the north. An old Marine Dictionary gives a nice definition of this manner of construction: "the disposition of the planks in the side of any boat or vessel, when the lower edge of every plank overlays the next under it, like the slates on the top of a house". In 1539/40, however, she had been completely rebuilt as the new type of warfare now developing at sea required entirely fresh thinking on ship construction and design. The *Great Harry* was now carvel-built in the fashion of the Mediterranean and of the Portuguese. (The word derives from the Caravel, a small, light, fast Portuguese ship which had opened up the Atlantic.) In carvel-building the planks are flush with one another. In northern latitudes the clinker method had been considered more suitable for local conditions, but Mediterranean carracks had long been carvel-built.

In 1546 the artist Antony Antony depicted the *Great Harry* as Henry VIII would have seen her as she led out the English fleet. She is different indeed. Now we see something that even Nelson would have recognized, for she has a square stern as compared with the old round sterns of the past, and her stern bristles with eight guns. The main difference, however, is that her sides are pierced with gunports, two tiers of them below the waist. The age of the broadside has begun and naval warfare has been revolutionized.

The great advantage of the flush-sided ship was that it had become possible to cut square gunports in the hull, which would permit square water-tight seals to be lowered and tightly closed on them when the ship was not in action. With the clinker-built hull, for obvious reasons, it would have been difficult to build efficient seals for the guns, as the construction would not have permitted it.

Whereas previously – since the advent of efficient heavy guns – the determining factor had been the amount of "gun weight" that could be carried on the upper deck, it was now possible to bring the guns down within the hull. The centre of gravity was thus lowered, and the ship could mount a great many more cannon than when they all had to be on the upper deck or thereabouts. It would seem that the *Great Harry* at this time was carrying about 130 guns made of iron, 21 heavy calibre bronze guns – her main armament – and a considerable number of hand guns. Sea warfare was in a change-over period and although the advent of heavy guns fore-shadowed the future of ship-to-ship actions at long range, allowance still had to be made for the old style boarding actions, where soldier fought against soldier.

The king would have looked across the grey waters of the summer Solent and seen a cloud of ships coming out of Portsmouth harbour. Unfortunately there

Previous page: A model of the Portuguese caravel. The word "carvel", describing a method of boat building with flush planking, derives from the caravels which were built in this way.

Left: An aerial view of Southsea Castle.

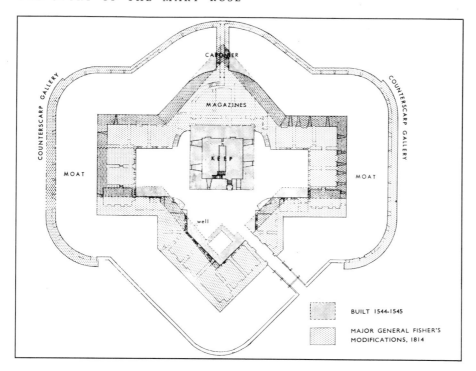

COUNTERSCARP GALLERY

COUNTERSCARP GALLERY

CANNONIER

MAGAZINES

KEEP

MOAT

MOAT

well

BUILT 1544-1545

MAJOR GENERAL FISHER'S MODIFICATIONS, 1814

Right: A plan of the castle showing later modifications to the original plan.

was very little wind and the great carrack-like warships were sluggish on the water. The attacking French, although having the advantage of sea-room, were little better off although they had sent probing ahead of them a number of galleys, for whom the untroubled sea provided ideal conditions. The English had never been inclined towards the galley, the rough and windy waters around their coasts making this descendant of the biremes of antiquity an unsuitable vessel, with its low free-board and its dangerously exposed oarports.

Emerging now from the press of English ships, and catching the king's eye for the sheer power and beauty of her appearance, was one of the greatest ships in all Henry's navy. This was the 700-ton *Mary Rose*. Pennons rustling in the light air, she flew the flag of a Vice Admiral, Sir George Carew. The king must have looked at her with pride. Although an old ship, she had been largely rebuilt nine years before, and she too, like the *Great Harry*, was now carvel-built. Her many gunports were all open, ready for the impending action, and cannons gleamed and glistened where they protruded from the darkness within. A splendid sight! Already, as the two fleets began to close one another, guns were beginning to bark over the still air. The French van preceded by the galleys was opening the action. The *Mary Rose* moved grandly forward. Fate waited in the wings.

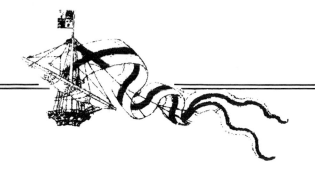

2. The Reason Why

IF THE French were now attempting to invade England, then the fault could very largely be laid at Henry's door. Ageing and sick though he was, he still aspired to the kingdom of France. Off and on throughout his reign, he and Francis I of France had been at war with one another. The French king remained, as now, Henry's major fear and the reverse was true for Francis, while the latter also had constantly to keep his eye on the Emperor Charles V.

Prior to the events of 1543 Henry VIII and Charles V had maintained an uneasy alliance, but the Emperor had deserted the English king and had even been appointed as a mediator between England and France. The quarrel between these rulers was, as always, a matter of power, land, money and fame. It was obscured by the smokescreen of religion – a very old and convenient means – for Henry naturally, since his break with Rome, supported the Lutherans on the continent and Charles the Catholics.

Charles as a Catholic (as well as Francis I of France) was disposed to – and did – lend aid to the Scots, those harriers of England's northern borders who themselves supported the old religion. Once again the fact that Henry had trouble on his northern borders was entirely of his own making. His father had managed to come to a *rapprochement* with Scotland, but Henry was not the man to tolerate a potential enemy in his backyard and, in his actions the year before this French invasion, had so infuriated the Scots that Archibald

Douglas, Earl of Angus, had been provoked to lead out a Scottish raiding force and had inflicted a defeat on the English.

Such was the state on the chessboard in the spring of 1545 that France was preparing to send out by sea a force to land in the north-west of Scotland and another to land in the Borderlands to the east. At the same time, Francis I, freed from concern about his other borders by his peace with the Emperor Charles V, intended to invade England from the south-east. It was this invasion fleet which Henry now watched approaching his realm as he sat on his horse at Southsea. He was fortunate in one thing only – that the projected French landings in the north never took place. Henry had outstretched himself in his continental wars and at that moment he faced a continent that was either hostile or indifferent to his interests. He had no ally, and stood alone.

Between 1542 and 1547, the year he died, Henry's campaigns cost him in excess of two million pounds (an astronomical amount in terms of modern money). To try and recoup his finances Henry had resorted to economic stratagems which will be familiar to all who live in this century – forced gifts and forced loans and the debasement of the coinage. Sales of ex-monastic lands in the two or three years preceding this current French invasion had brought hundreds of thousands of pounds into the exchequer, while the

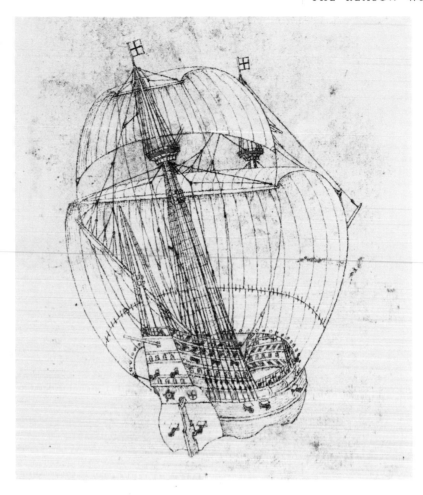

dissolution of various religious establishments that had hitherto escaped Henry's axe also yielded considerable sums. The king had subsequently cast his eye on church plate – a project which the Earl of Hertford applauded, remarking that "God's service, which consisteth not in jewels, plate or ornaments of gold and silver, cannot thereby be anything diminished, and these things better employed for the weal and defence of the realm". In addition to all this, the crown enjoyed a source of income from the secular Church. The considerable funds outlined above came, it must be remembered, over and above the standard income of the crown. Yet so much had his ships, his men, his castles cost him – let alone the expense of maintaining captured Boulogne as an English garrison – that Henry was still desperately short of money. His envoys were engaged in dealings with merchants on the Antwerp money-market in an endeavour to raise yet more.

Stephen Gardiner, Bishop of Winchester, was to write in 1545: "We are at war with France and Scotland, we have enmity with the bishop of Rome, we have no assured friendship here with the emperor and we have received from the landgrave, chief captain of the Protestants, such displeasure that he has cause to think us angry with him . . . Our war is noisome to our realm and to all our merchants that traffic through the Narrow Seas . . ."

This constant background of war, if it had done nothing else, had enabled Henry to build up a fleet that would prove the nucleus of all subsequent English sea-power. He had inherited, it would seem, seven ships from his father but this was little enough to cope with the demand of his continental wars. He had had his father's ship the *Sovereign* rebuilt in Portsmouth dockyard and shortly afterwards had had the keels laid of the *Mary Rose* and the *Peter Pomegranate*. Although no records of building have survived, it is

Above: The row-barge Floure
*e Luce, from the Antony
Roll.*

*Overleaf: An illustration of
he Galle Subtile from the
Antony Roll.*

probable that the *Mary Rose* was originally clinker-built, being converted to carvel in her massive refit in 1536. On the other hand, it is known that as early as the First French War (1513) English shipwrights had begun experimenting with the Mediterranean method of construction, as it was no secret that the Italians had already started to mount guns in the waists of ships, firing through gunports. This revolution in naval architecture was to lead to another one in tactics and sea warfare. The old floating platform, mounting light guns and man-killers like the serpentine, was to be displaced by ships like the *Mary Rose*, the ancestor of the ship-of the-line. At the Battle of the Nile and Trafalgar – and innumerable other engagements – similar ships were to give England the mastery of the sea. Aided by excellent gun drill, discipline and organization, this was to lead to that *Pax Britannica* which in its turn was to give the oceans of the world peace for close on one hundred

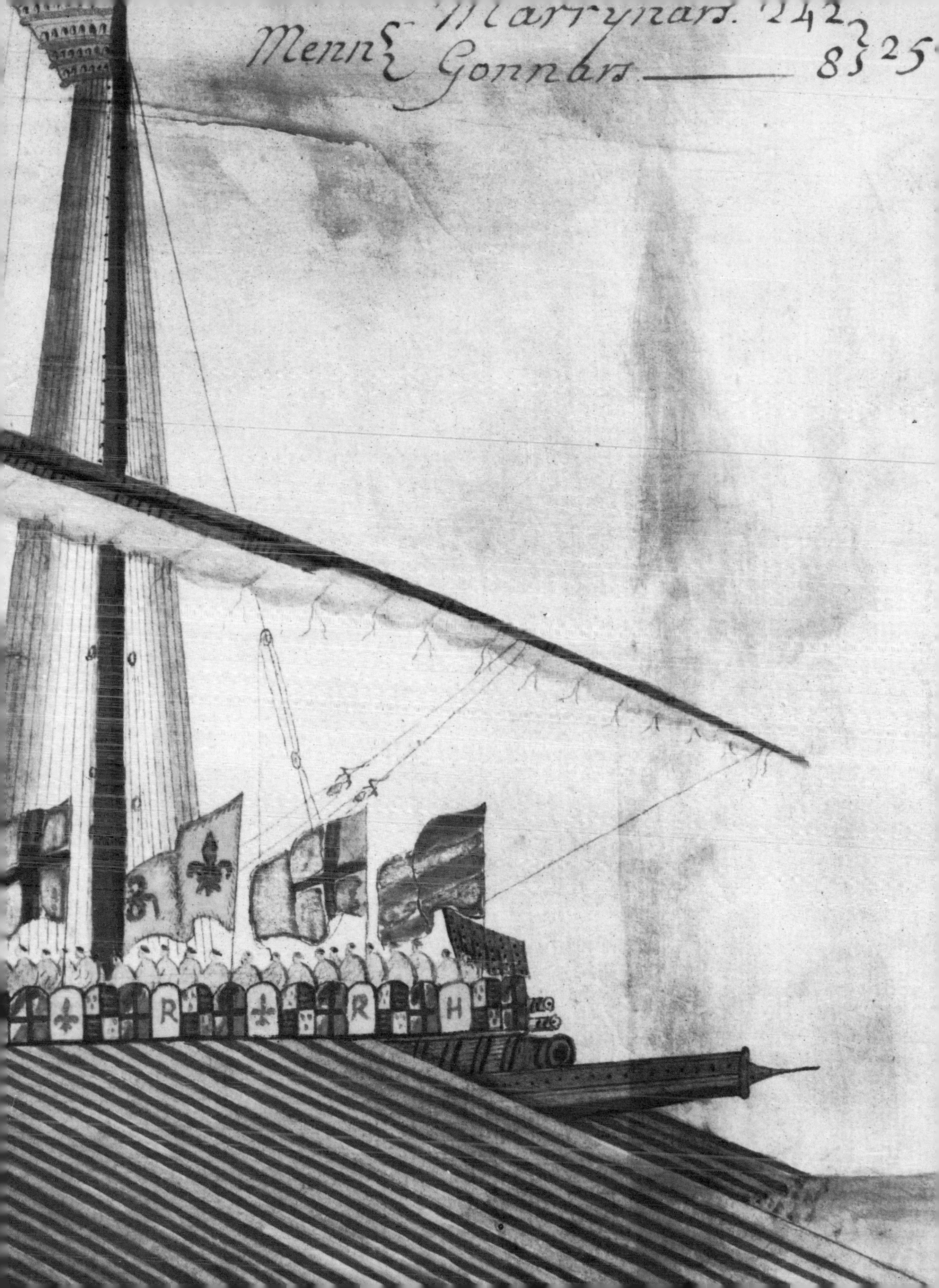
Menn
Marrynars 242
Gonnars 83
325
R
R
H

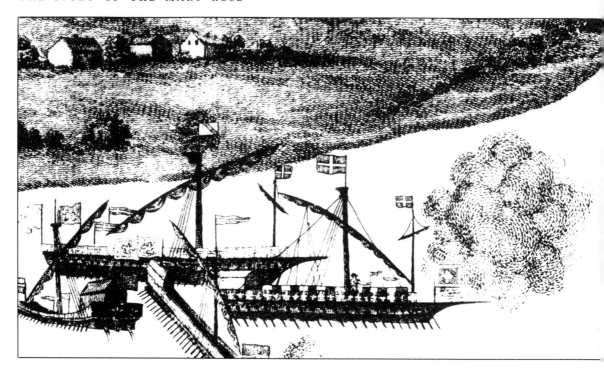

years. By 1514 Henry had increased his fleet by 24 ships, which he had later built up further, not only by home ship-building but by the purchase of Hanseatic and Italian vessels.

"Of all others," wrote Sir Julian Corbett (*Drake and the Tudor Navy*), "1545 best marks the birth of the English naval power: it is the year that most clearly displays the transition from oars to sails . . ." But the navy of Henry VIII had not entirely converted to the heavy sailing ship, for in this very action off Portsmouth the English made use of a type of composite vessel which employed both sails and oars. These Marshal du Bellay, who was with the French fleet and saw them in action on this July day, calls "ram-barges". The English term was "row-barge". There is a good picture of a row-barge *Cloud-in-the-Sun* in the Third Roll of the Antony Antony pictures of Henry VIII's navy. It is three-masted, rigged much like a pinnace, with squaresails on the fore and main and lateen on the mizzen. Sixteen oars aside, however, are set in the waist. It is armed with bow chasers, two heavy guns broadside under the half deck, and some carried stern chasers. Du Bellay describes row-barges as being even longer than galleys, narrow in the beam, and extremely agile in tideways and currents, of which the Solent can furnish plenty. To ships like the *Great Harry* and the *Mary Rose* they were much like destroyers were to battleships in the two World Wars.

detail from the Cowdray engraving, showing a skirmish between the Henry Grace à Dieu *and four French galleys.*

Later during this remarkable day in 1545, they were to give the French a great shock by suddenly emerging from the press of the English fleet and engaging the galleys which at that moment, by feigning a retreat, were trying to draw the English ships after them so that they could be annihilated by the great numbers of the French. (England opposed some 100 ships out of Portsmouth against 235 under the French Admiral.)

No doubt Henry VIII had already discussed with Viscount Lisle, the High Admiral, and Sir George Carew, the Vice-Admiral, the tactics to be adopted in view of the great preponderance of the enemy.

The eighteenth-century engraving made after a contemporary wall painting which was at former Cowdray House, Midhurst in Sussex, gives a panoramic and almost aerial view of the scene as the two fleets approached one another. Clearly there is very little wind for few have much, or any, sail set. The English fleet is coming out of Portsmouth some time after high water on the ebb tide. Viscount Lisle in the *Great Harry* is in the van and is engaging the four French galleys which, making use of the light weather, have been sent forward like gadflies to harass the English from a distance. No doubt the French design was to provoke their enemy so that they would all come out and engage in a general action, in which case the sheer numbers of the French

33

would have overwhelmed them. The English, not to be drawn, have anchored their heavier ships to the north of a channel leading towards the Isle of Wight, where they can if necessary command part of the entrance to Portsmouth harbour, while Southsea castle and the other defences command the more westerly approach.

The British aim was clearly to fight a holding action and either to lure the French into the deep channel where they would come under fire from Southsea Castle, or on to Hamilton Bank outside the harbour mouth. As the scene presents itself, only the High Admiral and Sir George Carew in their heavily-gunned, heavily-built ships were going to make an initial response against the French van, and give their galleys the taste of heavy metal. These two battleships could take anything that the bowchasers of the galleys could throw at them and, if the chance presented itself, one or two broadsides would blow the galleys out of the water.

As it happened, at the time that the Admiral's flagship got into action with the galleys she was only able to engage with her bowchasers. She possibly had the tide beneath her and only lightly northerly airs from astern, so there was no question of her having the manoeuvrability to bring her broadsides to bear. The galleys, on the other hand, were built for just such – almost Mediterranean – conditions. The *Mary Rose* was coming up well to port of the *Great Harry* and, to judge from the grouping of the lighter ships (including the row-barges), the intention was for these two strong men-of-war to lead out a double-headed attack on the French vanguard. Other vessels were also under way, including Sir Gawen Carew in *Matthew Gonnson*. It would be no more than a feint, however, for the size of the enemy armada precluded any greater scale of action.

Suddenly, amid the snap of the galley's light bowchasers and the boom of the forward guns on the *Great Harry*, the *Mary Rose*, which had not yet come into action, was seen to be in trouble. While in the process of hoisting her sails, and almost abeam of Southsea Castle, clearly intending to take advantage of a light wind which had begun to blow off the land, the *Mary Rose* became – in the sailors' words – snarled up. She began to heel over to port – and a heavy ship like her, with her high bow- and after-castles (let alone her weight of cannon) was not intended to heel like a racing yacht. She did not recover. Under the eyes of the king, his courtiers and the army gathered at Southsea, this pride of Henry's navy heeled even further until she dipped her gunports below the quiet, but always harsh, sea.

3. Death of a Ship

THE *Mary Rose* was finished from the moment that the sea began to rush in through her lower gunports. Within seconds the roaring waters would have become a torrent and her hold would have filled. There were no watertight bulkheads in those days.

What went wrong with this glorious Tudor ship?

First, at this point in naval architecture, the problems of rapidly sealing the gunports were hardly satisfactorily solved; and secondly, to judge from the Antony portrait of her, her 'tween decks battery were somewhat close to the water-line. Metacentric problems had in no way been clearly understood – it would be many, many years before they were – and no doubt the designers and the builders worked quite a lot on the value of eye-judgement. Since it was well enough known that heavy weights sited high up (on the upper deck, for instance) affected a ship's stability, the corollary may well have been assumed: the lower down the better.

Since the *Mary Rose* was just about to go into action it was natural that her gunports should be open. Indeed, a number of the guns, which have recently been salvaged, were shotted and primed, as was customary. This, of course, was very right and proper, and shows that the English were not just blundering out of Portsmouth, surprised and in a panic at the appearance of the French invasion fleet.

What first caused this great ship to heel over? Martin du Bellay in his *Memoirs* naturally ascribes it to French action: "Fortune favoured our fleet, in this manner, for above an hour, during which time, among many other damages which the English received, the *Mary Rose* one of their principal ships, was sunk by our cannon, and of the five or six hundred men which were on board, only five and thirty escaped."

This statement is highly suspect, not just because it is not corroborated by the English accounts, but because it goes against the grain of all naval likelihood. Only the French galleys were in action at that moment, and the only armament they could bring to bear were their comparatively light bowchasers, which would have done little enough harm to a ship of massive construction such as the *Mary Rose*. Furthermore the galleys were being engaged by the *Great Harry* – a great bear of a ship, swiping at rats with its forepaws – and at the long range their round shot would have had little or no effect upon the *Mary Rose*'s sides.

The *Mary Rose*, then, on the evidence of the Cowdray engraving at least, was so far to port of the *Great Harry* and of the preliminary action that she could not in any way have been affected by galley-fire. Had she blown up, because she had been struck in her vital magazines, then there would have been an explosion that would have been recorded by both sides – and which Henry VIII on Southsea Common would surely have witnessed. (Had she blown up, indeed, the underwater archaeologists would have long since registered the fact.)

No, the likelihood is that the *Mary Rose*, by the singular inadequacy of her ship-master – or the confusion and over-crowding aboard – was mishandled from the time that she began to get sail hoisted upon her. At the moment that she began to founder, the uncle of the Vice-Admiral, Sir Gawen Carew, had moved past in his own ship and had called out in consternation to his nephew – seeing that his ship was in difficulties – "*What is the trouble?*" In reply, Sir George Carew had called back: "*I have the sort of knaves I cannot rule.*"

What does this mean? Seamen, because of the hard and exploited nature of their calling, have been prone to mutiny over many centuries, but very rarely when going into action. "Lying in harbour," Nelson was to remark centuries later, "rots ships and rots men." This is true enough of the eighteenth century when, because of the long Anglo-French wars, ships were often kept in full commission during times of truce (on the chance that war might break out again at almost any moment). But the saying did not apply in the days of Henry VIII, when those eligible for military or naval service (whether peasants from the land or dwellers in the stews of the cities) knew well enough that some form of servitude was almost permanently their lot. Although, as in shipbuilding, the transition was at hand into that new

Sir George Carew, the Vice-Admiral of the Fleet, who sank with his ship, the Mary Rose. *The portrait is by Holbein.*

*Left and right: Two
engravings by Breugel (dated
circa 1560) showing
Mediterranean ships, with
rigs similar to the* Mary Rose,
under sail.

world heralded by the Italian Renaissance, it was still – especially in a
northern clime like that of England – essentially a Medieval world.

Whatever happened on that day will never be exactly known, but it is
clear that some gross mismanagement took place in the handling of the sails,
causing the *Mary Rose* suddenly to heel. The sailors and soldiers tumbled
down into the lee scuppers and, possibly, with them insufficiently secured
guns broke loose and hurtled across.

This sudden additional weight shifting down to the threatened side would
have been quite sufficient to put the lowermost gunports under the water.
Once that happened, as has been seen, total disaster was sure to follow. A
further clue to a possible cause of this tragic accident may well have been the
fact that the ship appears to have been grossly overmanned.

The normal complement of the *Mary Rose* was 415 men, yet du Bellay says
that there were 600 aboard, while Sir Peter Carew, the Vice-Admiral's
younger brother who left an account of the battle and the sinking (later used
by his biographer), says that there were 700 men aboard her that day. These
would not all have been mariners or gunners, who were part and parcel of the
ship's working complement, but must have been additional soldiers – archers,
billmen, pikemen, servants etc – put aboard in case the old-fashioned type of
boarding action should develop at some time during the battle. Now, to add

39

some 300 men to a ship which would have little enough space aboard even for her normal complement, and soldiers, moreover, unaccustomed to "the way of a ship in the sea", was to court disaster. A large number will have been on the upper deck, many of them in armour, and this additional weight, high up, would in itself have been sufficient to upset the *Mary Rose*'s stability. The sudden yawing of the ship as the sailors tried to handle the sails, doing this so ineffectively that she staggered as perhaps she altered course, would have been enough to precipitate armoured landsmen – without their sea legs – in a great tumble across the deck.

One who witnessed the sinking of the *Mary Rose* was Mary, the wife of Sir George Carew, the Vice-Admiral. She was standing in the company of Henry VIII, watching the progress of her husband's splendid vessel, when tragedy struck. Sir George Carew went down with his ship. So too did his captain, Roger Grenville. Hundreds of men drowned, some trapped below, others thrown into the sea, others sucked down in the water-coil of the sinking vessel, others no doubt tangled in rigging or stunned by falling spars, while the armoured men will have sunk like stones. In all, it would seem that only 35 men survived the wreck of the *Mary Rose*; some of them, perhaps, were men from the fighting tops who would have had the best chance of getting clear – if they could swim, and not many could do so in those days. No

Left: A detail from the
Cowdray Engraving showing
the French fleet off St. Helen's
at the entrance to the Solent.
Right. The scene of the
shipwreck. In the foreground
is Southsea Castle; the Mary
Rose sank in the middle
distance in line with the flag
on the Castle: In the far
distance the shore-line of the
Isle of Wight. The fort on the
left was built by Palmerston
in the 1860s to guard against
a later French threat.

personage of any importance managed to escape, and, not surprisingly, there is no record of the name of any humble sailor or soldier who was picked up by the small boats that were sent to the site of the wreck. Many would have been trapped and drowned in the anti-boarding netting.

The site of the wreck was clearly identifiable, as the Cowdray engraving shows; for the tops of her mainmast and her foremast protruded from the water. She had sunk in about six fathoms, and the fact that her masts showed so clearly above it (if the engraving is to be credited) indicate that it was some hours after the ebb when the English fleet was going out.

In the engraving, a man stands in the uppermost fighting-top of the mainmast, signalling for help. Drowned bodies float upon the Solent waters, and small boats are closing upon the wreck to pick up survivors. The cries of the drowning men and the shouts of the swimmers, hoping to be picked up, are said to have been heard by the king as he watched the events hard by Southsea Castle. (It seems likely that this would have been so: it was a quiet day and, quite apart from the fact that a light air was stirring off the land, noises across water are well known to be carried by that resonant sounding-board.)

It must have been a bitter moment for the king. All his life, since inheriting the throne, he had fought to make his island-kingdom great upon the continent, and to restore to it that image which had been forged by previous monarchs – Edward I, Edward III, and Henry V. The words had not yet been written, but they were already imprinted in Henry's heart:

> Then forth, dear countrymen: let us deliver
> Our puissance into the hand of God,
> Putting it straight in expedition.
> Cheerly to sea! The signs of war advance:
> No king of England, if not king of France.

It is easy, with the benefit of hindsight, to say that Henry VIII was wrong: that he should have never engaged in his continental wars; and that the future lay far away, across the Atlantic and across oceans then unknown. The king was a man of his time and (like most of us) he had been conditioned by the generations immediately before him.

Now, he would have gazed at the sunken ship and at the bodies of the dying or dead Englishmen: the end to which his policies had led him. It is worthless to conjecture – only to remember that he would have seen before him the widow of his Vice-Admiral, Carew, and heard the cries from the sea.

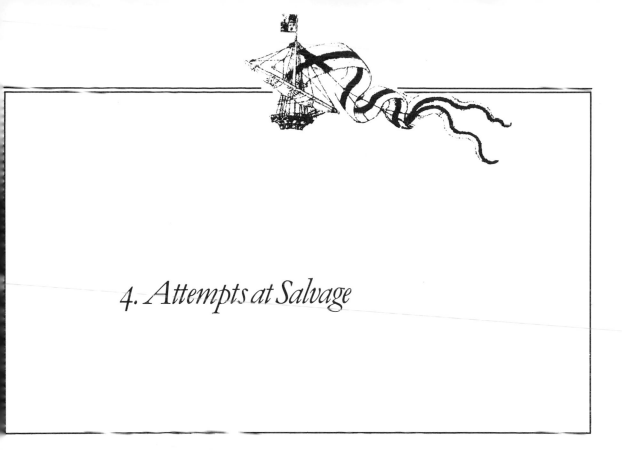

4. Attempts at Salvage

SINCE THE *Mary Rose* had sunk in midsummer, and since her position was clearly marked by her masts protruding above the water, it was natural enough that attempts should immediately be made to salvage her. So valuable a ship and with so great a weight of cannon aboard her could hardly be left to break up when the storms of winter hit the coast.

Diving as a means of recovering valuable treasures from the not too-deep "deep" was as old as the history of man and his navies. However, most of this diving had been done in the Mediterranean, where months of unruffled summer may follow one another, and in any case this was the "open" diving of swimming men who were as native to the sea as to their Aegean islands. The first known reference to mechanically-assisted divers occurs in Aristotle, who mentions instruments enabling the submerged man to draw air from above the water. Aristotle also writes of something similar to a diving bell, which was made of metal that did not fill with water but retained the air within it. This permitted the diver little freedom of movement and could only guarantee him a short time under the water since, as soon as the air above his head was exhausted, he had to return to the surface.

In the turbid waters of the Solent, neither the free diver nor the man in a primitive "bell" could have achieved much upon the wreck of a large ship and any idea of attempting to raise the *Mary Rose* would have been extremely

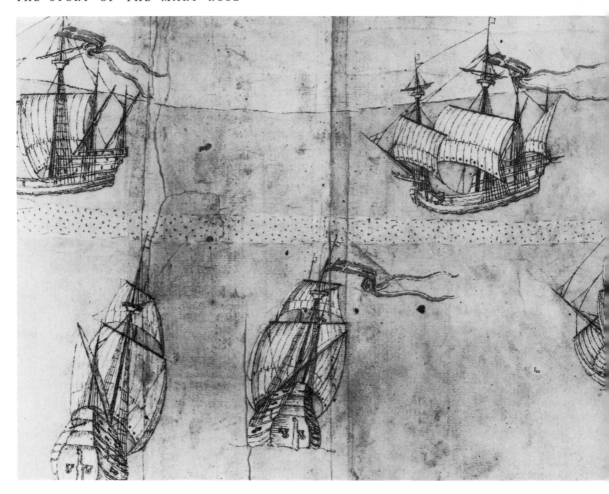

difficult. In any case, at that moment, the war was still in progress. The French, with their vastly superior fleet, were landing their troops on the Isle of Wight. They achieved little here, except the looting and rapine customary to troops of that time, and withdrew within a very short time. Their aim and ambition had been to capture Portsmouth as a reprisal for the English occupation of Boulogne and either effect an exchange or, if they had been able to make their landings in Scotland and the Border country, to close a pincer grip upon Henry's kingdom. It was clear now that the English, by "boxing canny", had foiled their foes from any attempt upon Portsmouth itself. The French had been prevented from destroying the English seaborne capability to maintain bases on the French sea coast, and the English now lay guarding the approaches, which they knew as well as fishermen know where lie their nets or their lobster-pots.

46

Men of war under sail in Calais Roads, from the drawing of 1545.

Writing to Sir William Paget on 23 July of that year Lord Russell commented:

> I am verie sory of the unhappy and the unfortunate chaunce of the *Mary Rose*: whiche through such rasheness and great negligence, soulde be in suchewise cast awaye, with thos that werr within herr which is a great loss of the Men, and the Shipp also, notwithstanding ye give me good hope by your letters that the Shipp shall be recovered againe, which I pray God may be so.

Unfortunately these sanguine expectations were to be disappointed, although it was not for the want of trying. Those masts – the tombstones of the *Mary Rose* and of the many men who had perished in her – were like a mocking invitation for men to try for her recovery. The Duke of Suffolk, also writing to Sir William Paget, itemized the requirements that would be necessary to raise the sunken ship:

> First two of the greatest hulkes that may be gotten more the hulkes that rideth within the haven. Item, four of the greatest hoys [small coasters, usually sloop-rigged] within the haven. Item, five of the greatest cables that may be had. Item, ten great hawsers. Item, new capstans with twenty pulleys. Item, fifty pulleys bound with iron. Item, five dozen ballast baskets. Item, forty pounds of tallow. Item, thirty Venetian maryners and one Venetian carpenter. Item, sixty English maryners to attend upon them. Item, a great quantity of cordage of all sorts.

The specific reference to Venetians serves as a reminder that at this date Venice was still the Queen of the Sea and more famous for its shipbuilding capabilities and marine know-how than any other state. In the event, the principal Venetian salvors engaged to attempt the raising of the *Mary Rose* were recorded as Petre de Andreas and Symone de Maryne (names that have clearly been anglicized). In view of relations with France and of the French naval superiority, concern was voiced by Viscount Lisle about withdrawing any ships from potential active service:

> The worst is, we must forbear three of the greatest hulks of the fleet till the thing is done, which must be emptied of all her vitayls, ordnance and ballast during the business, which will be a great weakening of the navy if anything in the meantime should happen.

Nevertheless, work went ahead and two carracks of the same size as the *Mary Rose*, the *Jesus of Lubeck* and the *Samson*, both of 700 tons, were stationed on either side of the sunken vessel. The aim was to lift her off the seabed using the buoyancy of these two ships and the rise of the tide (14 feet at springs). This could not have been achieved in one "lift" but would have required a series of them, on each occasion the hull being lightened as far as possible by the removal of guns and heavy gear. The trouble was, however, that the *Mary Rose* was not lying neatly in an upright position but was heavily heeled over. Ideally (which so rarely happens) cables would have been run under the sunken hull, running from one of the lifting vessels to the other so that each could have taken an equal strain. Before attempting to lift her the first thing to do was to get rid of her sails and yards – not only for their intrinsic value but because they would have made an infernal tangle, further complicating the task of the salvage parties. This preliminary work was completed by 5 August and the salvaged gear was sent ashore.

Now came the great test. Soon it was apparent that, with the *Mary Rose* lying at her awkward angle of heel, try as they might they could not effect

Opposite: Henry VIII, a Renaissance king in all his finery.

Overleaf: The only surviving contemporary picture of the Mary Rose, *taken from the Antony Roll, a list of King Henry VIII's ships completed in 1546. It shows the flagship after her rebuild in 1536.*

the juncture of the great cables under the hull with a satisfactory marriage to
each of the two lifting vessels. It was clear that there was only one recourse
and that was to attempt to bring the Mary Rose into something approaching
the vertical. The new capstans were manned; cables, hawsers and frapping
gear were made ready and at low water cables were made fast to her masts.
The hope was that, with the tidal lift, the salvage vessels would be able, by
carefully adjusting the cables, to exert a pull and bring the hull back into an
angle at which the real work of raising her could begin. Again they failed,
and all that happened was that the foremast was broken. By now it seemed
clear to Viscount Lisle that hopes of salvaging the Mary Rose were exhausted.
(She was a wreck that was beyond the technical capabilities of the time to
deal with.) A further suggestion was made by the Venetian salvors, that they
drag her as she lay into the shallows. How exactly they proposed to do this
with nothing more than manpower and the lift of the tide is difficult to see,
especially as she lay in soft silt. This last attempt also failed, the Venetians were
paid off, and the Mary Rose was abandoned.

On August 9 Viscount Lisle had other things to think about. Henry VIII,
who had previously ordered his fleet to remain passive at Portsmouth, had
decided to go over to the offensive. His High Admiral was ordered to take out
the fleet and give battle to the French who, after their foray into the Isle of
Wight, had made a somewhat similar landing at Seaford, withdrawing
shortly afterwards. (It is doubtful if Francis I, having failed to take
Portsmouth, ever intended his fleet to do anything more than harass the
south coast of England and cut the supply lines with Boulogne.) There was a
skirmish some six days later and the English fleet was left becalmed off
Beachy Head. Then a north-east gale blew up and Viscount Lisle was trapped
off Beachy Head (for a very different reason) while the French, taking
advantage of conditions favourable to them, took the wind under their sterns
and headed for home across the Narrow Seas. By September it was clear that
the invasion threat was over and the English fleet could prepare to winter in
Portsmouth.

By the end of the year Henry VIII was forced to admit to one of his leading
ministers that he was near bankruptcy. To such an end had his foreign wars,
his troops and ships brought him – and his kingdom – who at one time had
ruled what was probably the most financially stable country in Europe. On
Friday 28 January 1547, the king died.

The failure of the salvage operation did not mean that the Mary Rose was
forgotten: she was, of course, vivid in the memories of everyone in the fleet
as well as the inhabitants of Portsmouth. She was, to civilians and members
of the navy, somewhat similar to H.M.S. Hood in the Second World War, a
very well-known, old and famous ship, which had been heavily refitted for

53

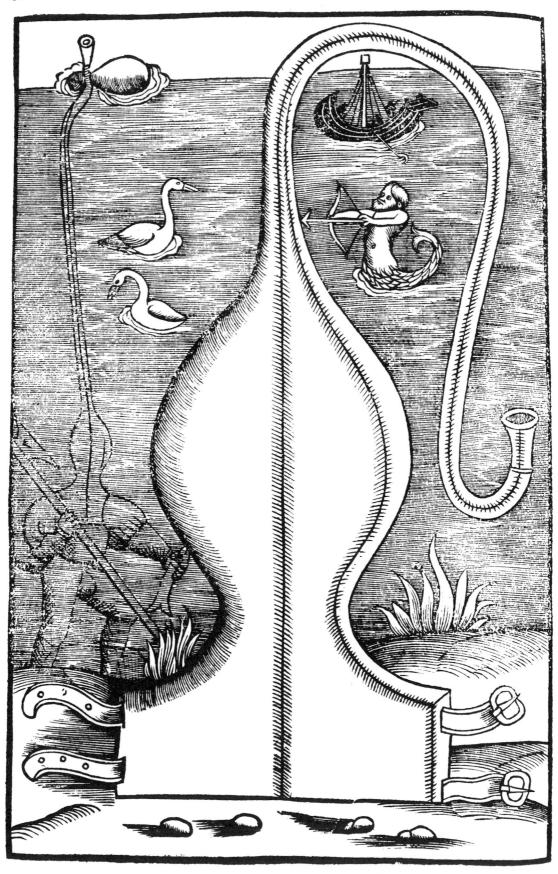

Left: This extraordinary
illustration was made for the
1532 edition of De Re
Militari, a military treatise
written in the fourth century
A.D. It shows the back view
of a helmet to be worn by a
soldier making an underwater
attack.
Above: Diving bells like this
were used for salvage work in
Spain in the sixteenth century.

the new conditions of sea warfare – but whose hull could not withstand the
demands that were made upon it. Unlike the *Hood*, the *Mary Rose* did not
sink in deep, cold waters far from her native island. That Italian divers were
still at work upon her wreck for some years after her sinking is evidenced by
the fact that a number of her guns were recovered within a few years of her
having sunk – those clearly discernible marks of her wreck – the fore- and
mainmasts – having disappeared beneath the far from pellucid waters of the
Solent.

There is no record of how these divers operated: it may have been from a
diving bell, lowered from a vessel above, from which vantage point they
would have had time to attach light lines around the barrels of guns, later
ascending to the surface with these and handing them to the men above, who
in their turn could have heaved around lifting hawsers from the decks of the
ship. On the other hand, it is possible that an individual diver was at work.
Mention is made of an Italian diver as being responsible for the salvage of
some of her guns. As early as the fourth century A.D. Vegetius, a somewhat
confusing writer on military subjects, who was nevertheless much revered in
the Middle Ages, had dealt with matters such as the attack on fortifications,
including those which were sited hard by the sea. In his *De Re Militari* (1532
edition in the British Museum) there is an engraving showing a diver wearing
a helmet to which is attached a long pipe of leather. This leads to the surface
of the water, at which point its open end is kept afloat by means of a bladder.
Such a system might have worked – to a very limited depth – in the lucent
waters of the Mediterranean in midsummer, but it seems a little unlikely that
it could have been much use in the unclear and tidal waters of the Solent.

The wreck was not forgotten, however, for a long time, since local line-
fishermen – knowing the predilection of fish for such areas – had her bones
well marked. That this was so is confirmed by the evidence of the
Elizabethan Admiral, Sir William Monson, who recorded in his *Naval Tracts*
(published in 1623) that he had been taken to the site of the *Mary Rose* and
there had seen "part of the ribs of this Ship . . . with my own eyes".

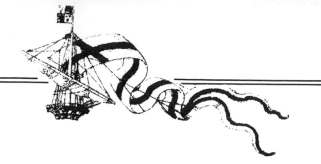

5. What Manner of Men?

"IT IS NOT the ship, but the men in her," runs an old Naval saying. Ships are ships – their character often depending upon their commanding officer – and some are crank, and some are good "sea boats", and some are bad even in harbour, and some can be fought to the end.

Sir George Carew had been Lieutenant-General of the Horse, and his appointment as Vice-Admiral had only just been made. His was a distinguished old family and his younger brother, Sir Peter, was to have his biography written by John Hooker. (It is from this we learn that about half the complement aboard the *Mary Rose* on that day were capable enough to be shipmasters in their own right: something which may well have led to the recorded confusion aboard – a case of "too many cooks".)

Sir George's captain, Roger Grenville, came from a Cornish family. His father had been Henry VIII's Marshal of Calais, while his four-year-old son – who witnessed the tragedy – was to grow up and also die a violent death at sea. One of the founders and preservers of the Virginia colony, Sir Richard Grenville (as he had become) was to engage some 15 Spanish ships off Flores in the Azores in Drake's *Revenge* – an exploit to be commemorated in Tennyson's ballad of that name.

The soldiers and sailors who perished in her went down nameless in the records of the event, although they, too, will have left widows and fatherless

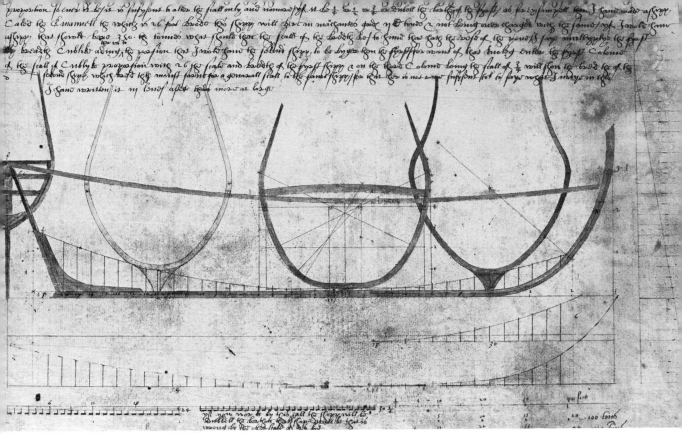

There are no plans of ships dating from the period of Henry VIII but this drawing from Fragments of Ancient English Shipwrights *in the Pepysian Library shows the draught of an Elizabethan ship with four sections.*

children. The word "sailor" was, indeed, not then in common usage, and the men who worked the ship were usually called seamen or mariners. At a later date, writing towards the close of the reign of Elizabeth, Sir Richard Hawkins made the precise distinction that the term *mariner* "ought not to be given but to the man who is able to build his ship, to fit and provide her of all things necessary, and after to carry her about the world; the residue to be but sailors."

One of the factors leading to trouble aboard the *Mary Rose* was an indiscipline resulting from matters of caste or rank. Drake, on his famous voyage round the world, had occasion, before entering the Straits of Magellan, to call all the men of the fleet together and to make an address which laid down for all time the rules that must obtain aboard ship:

Here is such controversy between the sailors and the gentlemen, and such stomaching between the gentlemen and the sailors, that it doth even make me mad to hear it. But, my masters, I must have it left, for I must have the gentlemen to haul and draw with the mariners, and the mariners with the gentlemen. What, let us show ourselves to be all of one company and let us not give occasion to the enemy to rejoice at our decay and overthrow.

The *Mary Rose* was overwhelmed in 1545, some thirty-three years before

57

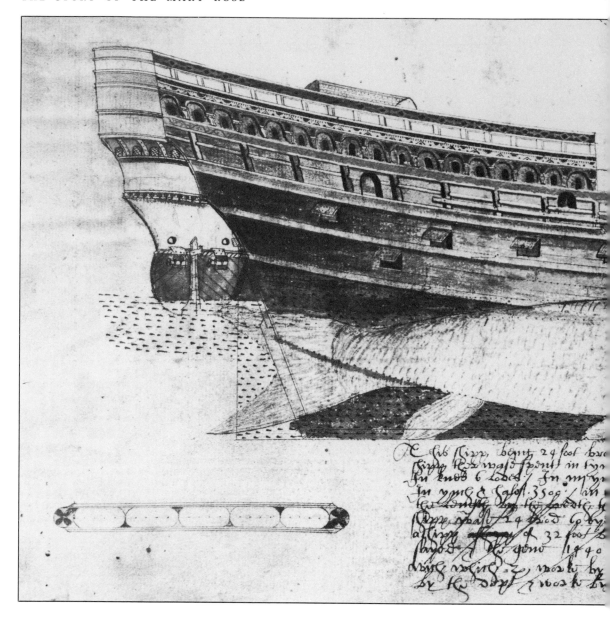

Francis Drake made that famous declaration; and in that time the whole aspect of sea-life had changed irrevocably. The navy of Henry VIII was still poised between the Middle Ages and the New World of the Renaissance: it was an uneasy transition. Not in literature, nor in music, nor in architecture, was the great change yet reflected: nor was it in shipbuilding, nor in the constitution of armies and navies. At that time it was certain enough that

A famous picture from Fragments of English Shipwrights, showing the draught of an Elizabethan ship compared to a fish. It will be interesting to compare the underwater lines of the raised hull of the Mary Rose with this later vessel.

"the gentlemen" would not haul and draw "with the mariners". Neither knew each other's trade, and the "gentleman" still felt assured that a sea-fight ended in a land-fight. In this the armoured men and archers, billmen and pikemen were supreme, and the mariners were only the rough handlers, of ropes, canvas and cordage, who drove them towards their destination.

Life at sea was extremely unpleasant – but so was life ashore. Impressment was still the mainstay of maintaining the manpower upon which the fleet was built, and impressment was still largely governed by provisions of a statute that had been laid down in the fourteenth century. As Christopher Lloyd (late Professor of History, Royal Naval College, Greenwich) observed in his book *The British Seaman*:

> Most of the provisions of the statute of 1379 were still in force early in the nineteenth century, but the penalty for desertion had increased to that of death . . . So were the provisions of the first Navigation Act passed in Richard's reign for the encouragement of that pool of seamen on which the Crown relied for the next four centuries. Other punishments laid down in the Laws of the Sea were more savage. Tarring and feathering, ducking and keel hauling were common for serious crimes. Nailing a man's hand to the mast, or cutting off his right hand for striking an officer or drawing a weapon, or binding a man to the corpse and throwing him overboard in cases of murder were probably less common.

For the offence of sleeping on watch, a man "shall be hanged on the bowsprit end of the ship in a basket, with a can of beer, a loaf of bread and a sharp knife, and choose to hang there till he starve, or cut himself into the sea." Such customs were still in force in the time of Henry VIII.

It was, however, in the reign of Henry VIII that the navy came to be regarded for the first time as a major weapon in the exercise of power and not just a means of transporting troops across to the continent. In 1546, the year after the wreck of the *Mary Rose*, Henry established the Navy Board at Deptford – Treasurer, Comptroller, Clerk of the Ships and Surveyor – thus establishing a framework which was to last well into the nineteenth century. The Ordnance Board, responsible for every aspect of guns, served both the army and the navy, while the Victualling Office, established in the reign of Elizabeth, provided the headquarters not only for victualling the ships, but for paying the officers and men, maintaining the vessels, building them, and manning them.

It was in this quarter, victualling, that most of the troubles arose over the centuries; for it was naturally in this area that there existed opportunities for corruption and dishonesty. The victualling of a ship like the *Mary Rose* was organized by contract with the purser aboard and wholesalers ashore. The ration per man as laid down in 1545 was a pound of biscuit, a pound of meat and a gallon of beer for four days every week, while for the other three days the allowance was dried fish and cheese. If the crew did in fact receive their true rations then they were considerably better off than many a farm labourer or townsman ashore. Their pay early in the reign of Henry VIII had been five shillings a month, but this had been raised in the king's later years

Above: Gold angel coins found in the Mary Rose.
Overleaf: This painting by Holbein shows Henry VIII presenting a charter to the Guild of Barber Surgeons who are seen wearing their characteristic caps, one of which was found aboard the Mary Rose.

to six shillings and eight pence as a reward for long and honest service. (However, this raise – as we have seen so often in our own times – had been nullified by the devaluation of the shilling to the equivalent of six pence.) The gold coins known as "angels" (angel-noble), which have been found inside the ship, were worth six shillings and eight pence, and were at the time a day's pay for the Vice-Admiral. The Tudor seaman was familiar with that other problem of our time – inflation; but some idea of contemporary prices can be judged from the fact that a pair of leather shoes could be bought for five pence.

Soldiers' uniform cost about four shillings a head, twice that of seamen. Militia men wore jackets of green and white cloth or – at a somewhat later date – linen baggy breeches. If they wore head gear at all it was either high, thrum caps with a peak, or flat woollen tam o'shanters.

In the overcrowded condition of the ships it was not surprising that, with low standards of hygiene, disease was rife. Venereal disease was common; syphilis, "the great pox", having made vast inroads throughout Europe in the sixteenth century. Bubonic plague, carried by rats, was endemic in the society of that time. In the very year that the *Mary Rose* sank, a letter from the admiral aboard the *Great Harry* referred to "a great disease fallen among the soldiers and mariners almost in every ship, in such sort that if the same

should continue, which God Forbid, we should have need to be newly refreshed with men''.

Many centuries later (in 1812) a clergyman, Edward Mangin, wrote as follows:

So I bid adieu to the sameness and (to me) insupportable vexations of a naval life; to the necessity of dwelling in a prison; within whose limits were to be found Constraint, Disease, Ignorance, Insensibility, Tyranny, Sameness, Dirt and Foul Air; and, in addition, the dangers of Ocean, Fire, Mutiny, Pestilence, Battle and Exile.

Admittedly, the reverend gentleman was clearly unfitted for the sea-life, but one wonders what he would have made of life aboard a Tudor warship like the *Mary Rose*.

Medical knowledge and practice were very limited at the time that this great ship sailed to her death – and in any case, so sudden was it, that it would have little benefited anybody aboard if it had been. The Company of Barber-Surgeons was required by charter to provide men on request when ships were in active commission, and we know that one of them was present aboard the *Mary Rose*. Although the College of Physicians was already established, almost no members served afloat – for the very obvious reasons that life at sea was so dirty and dangerous and unrewarding. The Barber-Surgeons were a lower degree of doctor altogether, and it was not until the nineteenth century that the dispute between these two branches of the medical profession was resolved. The Barber-Surgeon who served aboard the *Mary Rose* was probably pressed into service, and it is unlikely that his medical and surgical knowledge went far beyond the treatment of venereal disease and rudimentary surgery. The medieval mariner had, in some respects, been better cared for than those in the reign of Henry VIII; for the king had dissolved the old charities which cared for them when wounded or sick.

It was not until some twenty-three years later that there was to appear the official *Orders to be used in King's or Queen's Majesties Ships or Navy being upon the Seas in Fashion of War*. This laid down simple fighting instructions: the principal advice being that, having overcome and seized an enemy ship, only the captain and other notables should be taken prisoner – the rest being sunk with their ship ''for else they will turn upon you to your confusion''. There were specific punishments for swearing and blasphemy, as well as simple instructions for fire control. The captain, for instance, is advised to have two large casks chained to the ship's sides ''for the soldiers and mariners to piss into that they may always be full of urine to quench fire with and two or three pieces of old sail ready to wet in the piss''. As has been said, notions of hygiene were primitive in the extreme, with the result that, if ever the fleet was manned for any length of time, disease was sure to take its toll. M. Oppenheim (*History of the Administration of the Royal Navy*) calculates that in 1545 out of a total of 12,000 soldiers and sailors 3,502 either died or had to be discharged sick due to an outbreak of plague. It is perhaps significant that among so many other evidences of death aboard the *Mary Rose* – the skeletons of men – there have been found the bones of a black rat, that carrier of the plague-bearing flea.

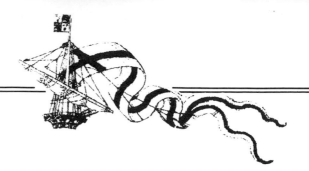

6. The Sinking & After Effects

MYSTERY SURROUNDS the loss of the *Mary Rose*. It is a mystery that may possibly be solved when what remains of her hull is brought to the surface – but it is equally likely that she took to the seabed, along with her recalcitrant mariners, the secret of her loss. What is strange about the Cowdray engraving depicting the action between the English and the French on that July day is that such wind as there is appears to be coming off the land. But perhaps one should not make too much of this for, although clearly designed to be as accurate as possible, the ways of artists with the sea and ships have often provoked the wrath of naval men.

If the wind was indeed offshore then it is difficult to understand how the tragedy happened, for hoisting squaresails under such conditions should have been comparatively easy. Tacking with squaresails was another matter altogether and, with a crew who had not worked together before or where there were too many "masters" and not enough straightforward hands, it can be seen that something might have gone seriously wrong – as it obviously did. But another mystery remains: the direction of the ship's head.

As is clear from the engraving and from what we know of fleet tactics as introduced during Henry's reign, the English ships are going out in two main columns – that on the right (the battall) led by the High Admiral of England, Viscount Lisle, in the *Henry Grace à Dieu*, while the port column (the

vauverde) is being led by the Vice-Admiral, Sir George Carew, in the *Mary Rose*. So light is the wind that many have not hoisted sail, and they are clearly coming out on the ebb tide. Two masts of the *Mary Rose* are visible beyond Southsea Castle, indicating where she has sunk.

In the fighting top of the mast which is nearest the shore the figure of a man is visible, waving frantically for help. Is this survivor on the foremast or the mainmast? If he is in the fighting top of the foremast then the *Mary Rose* is pointing north to Portsmouth, if he is in the top of the mainmast then she is outward bound towards the French. Even a close examination of the engraving provides no clues. From Sir Peter Carew's account of the disaster in which his elder brother met his death it seems clear that when his uncle, Sir Gawen Carew, sailed up alongside the *Mary Rose* and inquired of the Vice-Admiral what was the matter (to receive the now famous reply "I have the sort of knaves I cannot rule") the *Mary Rose* was in the port van. So remarkable a thing as the Vice-Admiral turning about in the face of the enemy could never have gone unrecorded and du Bellay's comment that the *Mary Rose* was "sunk by our cannon" must remain suspect. That some incompetence and failure in handling the sails, coupled with the weight and movement of several hundreds of soldiers in her fore and after castles, led to her dipping her gunports into the sea must be seen as the cause for her loss.

As Sir Julian Corbett wrote in *Drake and the Tudor Navy* (1):

> . . . it is abundantly clear that under Henry VIII the English Navy was becoming an entirely new thing, a thing the world had never seen before. With ample resources to have anything he wanted, in face of Italian, Spanish, and even French opinion, he chose to create a Navy which ignored the vessel that all ages had regarded as the ideal capital ship [the oared galleasse or the galley], and to reduce the rowing vessel to entirely subordinate functions, to place it in fact in much the same position as that which a torpedo-boat holds today.

The *Mary Rose* was the wave of the future at that time, and only the fact that she was still in a transition stage between the great carrack of the past and the smaller vessel of the Elizabethan Age can serve to enable someone of the twentieth century to understand exactly how important she was. It is as if, in the long history of mammalian evolution, we could detect at exactly what point the ape that was not quite a man, turned the corner and suddenly became a tool-making creature.

In the first half of the sixteenth century a book by a Spaniard, Alonso de Chaves, reveals that sailing tactics and strategy had been carefully studied and that "the state of the art" was not just a primitive form of laying one's ship alongside and boarding the enemy. It was hardly surprising that such a volume should have issued from Spain, for that country was well on the way to becoming the richest empire in the world, through its grasp upon the New World to the west, which inevitably meant through its superior knowledge of the sea and sea warfare. This of course was to be hotly disputed in the seas and oceans of the world during the reign of Queen Elizabeth (culminating in the defeat of the Armada). But the foundations of English oceanic voyaging had already been laid in Henry's reign. William Hawkins of Plymouth (a man whom Hakluyt says was much loved and esteemed by the king) by his voyages to Brazil and Guinea had pointed the way for future navigators. In 1540 Robert Reniger or Ronnyger followed in the wake of Hawkins to the New World. It is interesting to note that in the campaign of 1545 there were two captains with the name of Ronnyger and both furnished ships for the king's cause. (It has been argued that this was a clerical error, and the same man was put down twice.)

As early as 1532 the king had instructed Thomas Audley, later Lord Chancellor, to draw up a set of orders for the conduct of His Majesty's forces both by land and sea. Audley undoubtedly drew on all the expert knowledge then available, but this was still prior to the advent of the big gun ship like *Mary Rose*. This is made clear by such instructions as: "If they chase the enemy, let them that chase shoot no ordnance till he be ready to board him,

for that will let [hinder] his ship's way." Boarding was at that time still the main purpose of an action: "In case you board, enter not till you see all the smoke gone, and then shoot off all your pieces, your port-pieces, the pieces of hailshot and cross-bar shot to beat his cage-deck; and if you see his deck well rid, then enter with your best men, but first win his top in any wise if it be possible."

By 1545 with a ship like the *Mary Rose* being armed with 91 breech loading and muzzle loading guns, and capable of a full broadside, the old fighting instructions were already out of date. Yet the very fact that she had so many soldiers and archers aboard her suggests that the concept of boarding had certainly not been discarded, while the light moveable boards above the gunwale were not only to protect the gunners and archers from hostile fire, but also to prevent the enemy storming aboard. So, too, was the use of netting designed to obstruct an enemy trying to swarm over the side. Unfortunately, on that day when the *Mary Rose* rolled over and sank, such precautions taken to prevent the enemy boarding must have held up and caught many of her own crew and stopped them from getting out in time from the sinking ship.

Not long after the Battle of Portsmouth King Henry VIII seems to have had a change of heart about his Channel Navy. No doubt the sudden and inexplicable sinking of his rebuilt warship, from which he had hoped great things, had had a searing effect on his opinions. He was an old man now, and old men, whatever the innovative vitality of their youth, tend to return to conservative principles. Henry had been discomforted to see the ease with which the French Admiral had been able to flout his larger ships on a calm day. He determined that, whatever great ships he might have, he must also have an oared squadron for use on any similar occasion, to put his fleet on equal terms with the French.

Viscount Lisle, who was already fully occupied with providing the men and ships to assist the Venetians in their attempts to raise the *Mary Rose*, was now given the added burden of forming this new squadron of light ships; principally, though not entirely, oared. The row-barges, which had shown themselves useful in the Battle of Portsmouth, were clearly not considered sufficiently seaworthy to accompany the fleet far out into the Narrow Seas. It is to the credit of Lisle, and the shipwrights and other craftsmen who worked for him, that he had this squadron of galleasses and pinnaces ready by the middle of August. Earlier he had written to Paget: "Whereas the King's Majesty's pleasure is to have certain of his ships brought to pass to row, to keep company with others of that sort to attend upon the French galleys, there shall be as much done unto it as stuff and time will serve to perform the same."

Previous page: A famous painting of a four masted Portuguese carrack, thought to be the Santa Caterina do Sinai, *dated circa 1520. The ships in the foreground are, in fact, different views of the same vessel. The harbour in the background is Naples. The huge mainsail was a characteristic feature of the great carracks.*

70

In the second half of the sixteenth century the design of fighting ships changed. Gradually those high forecastles and aftercastles – relics of an earlier age – became trimmed down. A fighting ship with a far lower profile emerged, one that will be seen in the age of Elizabeth I. The vast amount of windage represented by these castles was now seen by mariners and master shipwrights alike as a great source of danger – as well as reducing sailing qualities. A ship like the *Mary Rose*, as shown in the Antony Antony Roll, would have been as difficult to manoeuvre or keep on course as a barn, in anything approaching a beam wind. What was to emerge as the future hull form tended to have a relatively low forecastle, a long beakhead, a steved-up bowsprit, and an aftercastle which, though prominent, has nothing of the ostentation of the earlier ships. To make a comparison between the *Mary Rose* and a ship of Drake's time is rather like looking at a famous make of motorcar as it was in 1914, and then seeing where evolution, experience and technology have taken it 60 years or more later. The unhappy Spanish Admiral, the Duke of Medina Sidonia – as the Armada struggled up Channel in 1588 tormented by the gadflies of the lower-profiled English ships – wrote in a despatch: "The heaviness of our ships, compared with the lightness of theirs, rendered it impossible in any manner to bring them to close action . . ."

"Of all others the year 1545 best marks the birth of the English naval power . . ." wrote Sir Julian Corbett. One may well agree, even though it marks the sinking of the ill-fated *Mary Rose*, for it was the year in which the French attempt on Portsmouth – in revenge for the English capture of Boulogne – was thwarted. Thwarted, too, was the attempt of the French Admiral to lure the smaller English fleet out into open water, where his far larger numbers should have decimated the English, leaving the way to Portsmouth open. When the French were finally scattered and, disillusioned, made their way back to France, it could be seen as a year of triumph.

Yet the fact remains that, after the Battle of Portsmouth, Henry no longer put all his faith in the large sailing ship. It now became a two-tier navy. First and foremost remained the heavily gunned sailing vessels, but with them when they put to sea went a force of oared vessels. Thus, to put it in the terms of Nelson's navy, along with the ships deemed heavy enough for the line of battle, went a light squadron which might be likened to the later frigates. In the terms of the two World Wars of the twentieth century, these were the fleet destroyers that provided the screen for the battleships.

Mr. Nicholas Braddock, who has made a specialized study of the battle, and of the number of English ships involved on that day, has come to the conclusion (based on the *Letters and Papers Foreign and Domestic Henry VIII*

1545) that the total of the English fleet which came out from Portsmouth was 105. This agrees with Peter Carew: "the resydue of the fleete, being aboute the number of one hundred and fyve sails, take the seas." The Cowdray engraving, as Mr. Braddock points out, shows 51 but the bunching at the harbour entrance implies more coming out.

I must agree with Thomas Hardy in *The Dynasts*: "My argument is that War makes rattling good history; but Peace is poor reading." Had the *Mary Rose* been like many a British warship in the second half of the nineteenth century which kept the *Pax Britannica* upon the seas and oceans, but never saw action, she would have been forgotten. Had she not been refound, and excavated with all the archaeological and scientific skills of the twentieth century, a great gap would have existed in our knowledge of Tudor ships and the Tudor seaman.

The English seaman in the reign of Henry VIII was still a comparative newcomer to the art of navigation – especially of deep-sea work. He was an excellent pilot but his pilotage was often that of the fisherman – from whom it stemmed – being a compendium of local knowledge and early acquired skills in small boats off familiar shores. As late as 1625, one English captain (Luke Foxe), was bold enough to write that he had no use for "mathematical seamen".

> . . . I do not allow any to be a good seaman that hath not undergone the most offices about the ship, and that hath not in his youth been both taught and inured to all labours; for to keep a warm cabin and lie in sheets is the most ignoble part of a seaman; but to endure and suffer, as a hard cabin, cold and salty meat, broken sleeps, mouldy bread, dead beer, wet clothes, want of fire, all these are within board; besides boat, yard, top-yards, anchor-moorings and the like.

One hears here the voice of the "salt-horse", as he compares his knowledge and his lot with that of the "boffin".

The Frenchman Pyrard who is quoted in Hakluyt, went to India in 1601 and returned in a great Portuguese carrack in 1610. He writes:

> After the captain the pilot is the second person in the ship for the master obeys him and does as he orders. He never leaves his place on the poop ever observing the needle and compass, he has a second pilot to help him. The master is after him and commands the seamen ordinary seamen and others who work the vessel he has a mate under him to help him, these are all appointed by the King. The master's duty is to command from the poop to the main-mast. The master's-mate takes charge from the forecastle to the foremast inclusive of that mast and has the same duties there as the master

on the poop . . . The mariners are highly respected and there are few of them but can read and write such being very needful to them for the art of navigation. For by this word mariners is to be understood one who is well instructed in navigation, but yet there are few good at it although all bear the name. Theirs is the work of steering the ship each in his turn. In these great ships they take 1 or 2 ordinary seamen to their aid. They do all the work that has to be done aloft such as setting and reefing the sails. [This would be on a long passage when there was little sail handling to be done]. They never clean the ship nor work the pumps save when necessity requires. It must be noted that in these large ships there must be 3 compasses [it is a coincidence that three compasses have been found aboard the *Mary Rose*]; the pilot that is high up on the poop has one, under the deck there is another for the mariner who is there to hear the pilot, because he that is below at the helm could not hear him; so the one that is betwixt passes on to him the pilot's word.

The arrangements aboard the *Mary Rose* may not have been so dissimilar: "The rudder-stock reached to the lowest of the 3 decks in the stern-castle; here was the tiller and helmsman with a compass before him; on the deck next above was a mariner with a compass before him to pass the pilot's orders to the helmsman and on the highest deck the pilot also with a compass."

Aboard the Portuguese vessels a sergeant was appointed to execute "the commands of the captain in matters of justice" and a military officer or a sergeant may well have fulfilled the same function aboard the *Mary Rose*.

The sergeant has also charge of the fires. For this purpose there are on the 2 sides of the ship at the main-mast 2 large kitchens; when the sergeant lights the fire there which is close upon 8 or 9 o'clock there are always 2 guards present one at each kitchen. Also he has the duty of seeing the fires put out which is at about 4 o'clock. On these vessels are also many artisans, surgeons carpenters caulkers coopers etc; all the ship's officers have each his own station . . . The master mate guardian and master-gunner have each a big silver whistle wherewith they make known all their orders.

One galley only has been found aboard the *Mary Rose*, probably all that was needed in the comparatively short voyages which she was called upon to make, but it can be assumed that similar marked attention was given to the lighting and the dousing of the fire – that most dangerous of elements in ships which were built of wood and filled with gunpowder. Silver whistles with which orders were given aboard ship have been found in the *Mary Rose*, and indeed have continued in use in the Royal Navy right into the twentieth century. Their purpose now is mainly for ceremonial use, but in the age of sail they were the most efficient means of communicating orders.

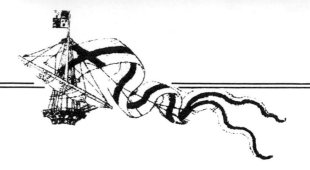

7. The Lost Centuries

AFTER THE record of Sir William Monson's sighting of the wreck of the *Mary Rose*, she seems to vanish from the chronicles, although she will have taken a little longer to disappear from folklore. Portsmouth, then, was a small town, and small towns have long memories.

Forty-three years after Henry VIII's great ship had sunk, the Channel to the south of her grave witnessed the greatest procession of ships that those waters had ever seen – the "Enterprise of England", the Spanish Armada, was passing to the eastward, harried by the ships under Admiral Howard. It was some ten miles east, where the Owers lie – those shoal banks toothed in places by rocks – that Drake launched an attack on the seaward wing of the Spanish fleet, hoping no doubt to force the enemy upon this formidable hazard. (The pilot to the Spanish Admiral, Medina Sidonia, had indeed already reported shoals to port when a shift of wind enabled the Armada to draw offshore and head for Calais.) So many of those great ships were quite soon to share the fate of the *Mary Rose* – their bones scattered round the coasts of Scotland and Ireland. (There were in fact fewer ships in this Spanish Armada than there had been in the French invasion of 1545.)

It is significant that the bulk of the English fleet now came from Plymouth in the West, for, in less than half a century, the attention of the Elizabethan mariner had shifted to the Atlantic and the new lands far away. The great

Right: location of the wreck of the Mary Rose, *superimposed upon a chart of 1759 in Portsmouth Museum and Art Gallery.*

74

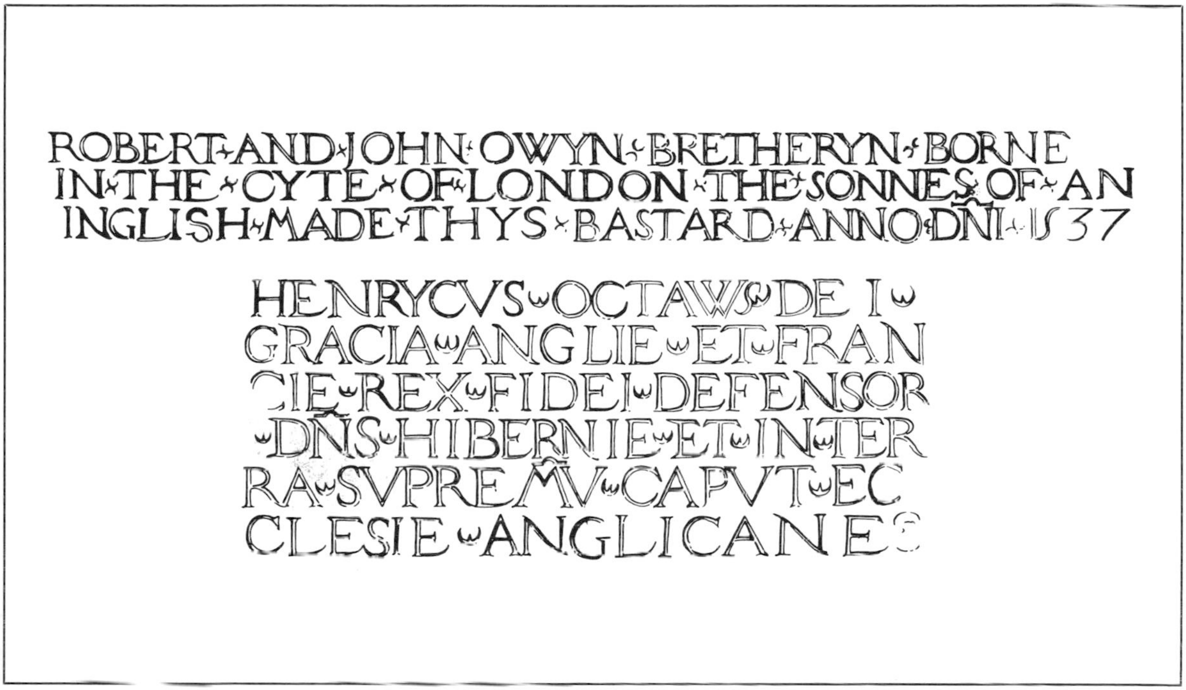

ROBERT·AND·JOHN·OWYN·BRETHERYN·BORNE
IN·THE·CYTE·OF·LONDON·THE·SONNES·OF·AN
INGLISH·MADE·THYS·BASTARD·ANNO·DÑI·1537

HENRYCVS·OCTAWS·DE I
GRACIA·ANGLIE·ET·FRAN
CIE·REX·FIDEI·DEFENSOR
·DÑS·HIBERNIE·ET·IN·TER
RA·SVPREMV·CAPVT·EC
CLESIE·ANGLICANE

Left: Between 1836 and 1840 John Deane, seen here working on the wreck of the Royal George, salvaged a number of guns from the Mary Rose.
Right· Two beautiful inscriptions on one of the guns salvaged from the Mary Rose.

enemy now was Spain, and France – though hardly a friend – had become of secondary importance.

The many wars fought upon those Narrow Seas, fought between the continental powers and the obstinate offshore island, constitute much of the history of the English Navy, which in itself is much of the history of England. They pass like the annual drift of leaves in autumn. Over the *Mary Rose*, herself one of the principal progenitors of the Navy, year by year, and century after century, passed the drift, and the steady fall of sand, silt and mud from the Solent.

The *Mary Rose*, like some Egyptian Pharaoh, was being embalmed – and encapsulated – by the currents and tidal effect of her native sea.

Once again the war was with France. Out from Portsmouth came the descendants of the *Mary Rose*. Mounting the broadside guns which the *Mary Rose* and the *Great Harry* had more or less pioneered, a ship like the *Victory*, which now hauled out for that conclusive naval battle at Trafalgar, was built also, very largely, of native oak. The *Victory*, carrying Nelson to his last sea-battle, was the perfection of warship sailing-design. Mounting some 100 guns, she was approximately 2,200 tons: 186 feet long on the waterline, with an extreme beam of 52 feet; her draught was about 21 feet. She and others like her sailed past the grave of their ancestor. A second-rate would be 170 feet

77

long; a third-rate, 160 feet; these classes formed the Navy's battle fleet.

The thunder of propellors took over from the roar or rustle of canvas. First coal- and then oil-fired boilers drove the new metal-clad ships – towards another foe from across the Channel. For the first occasion in centuries that enemy was not from just across the Narrow Waters, but from distant Germany. It made little difference. Out of Portsmouth, as they had done for centuries, moved the ships that defended the coastline of their country.

By the time of the First and Second World Wars the *Mary Rose* had been quite forgotten – though she had been rediscovered in the nineteenth century. The story of this first rediscovery has been admirably told by Alexander McKee in his *History Under the Sea* (Hutchinson, 1968) – and Mr. McKee was very largely responsible for her second rediscovery. All this was consequent upon the ingenuity and courage of two men, Charles and John Deane, who became – not as the tale relates the first "divers" – but the first scientifically-minded ones. In *History of Three Kent Parishes* R. H. Goodshall wrote that: "Whitstable was the birthplace of the diver. The first man to go underwater was John Deane . . ." He became a diver through a curious concatenation of circumstances, the first being that he was present at a farm when a fire occurred and some valuable horses were trapped in a stable. All efforts to save them including the use of a primitive water-pump having proved unavailing, John Deane, who knew that in the farmhouse "stood an old suit of armour", asked the farmer "if he might use the helmet and try to save the horses. Consent was readily given, and placing it over his head, he secured the pipe from the old pump and asked the farmer to pump air slowly. Then, he walked into the stable through the dense smoke, and brought out one horse after another, until all were saved."

What has all this to do with the *Mary Rose*? Everything. From discovering the use of a metal helmet with an air supply Deane went on to the business of diving on wrecks – always a profitable custom around the rocky coasts of England. Having tested his skills on simple diving for anchors, he was then "encouraged to try a bigger job. A suitable wreck he considered was the *Royal George*, which sank at Spithead on 28 August 1782. He took with him the ingenious apparatus which he had invented and improved. He now had a rubber dress, made perfectly water-tight, and a helmet large enough for him to turn his head round at pleasure, having three glasses to admit light, and a flexible rubber tube on the top to supply air from above by means of an air pump, worked by a man in attendance."

By such means did John Deane discover the *Mary Rose*. During the years 1834 to 1836 the two Deane brothers had been diving on the wreck of the *Royal George* – a famous ship-of-the-line of 108 guns which had gone down not for reasons of war or fire, but because of structural failure. During the

A watercolour painting from John Deane's book Cabinet of Submarine Recoveries, Relics and Antiquities, *showing some of the guns salvaged by the Deane brothers from the* Mary Rose.

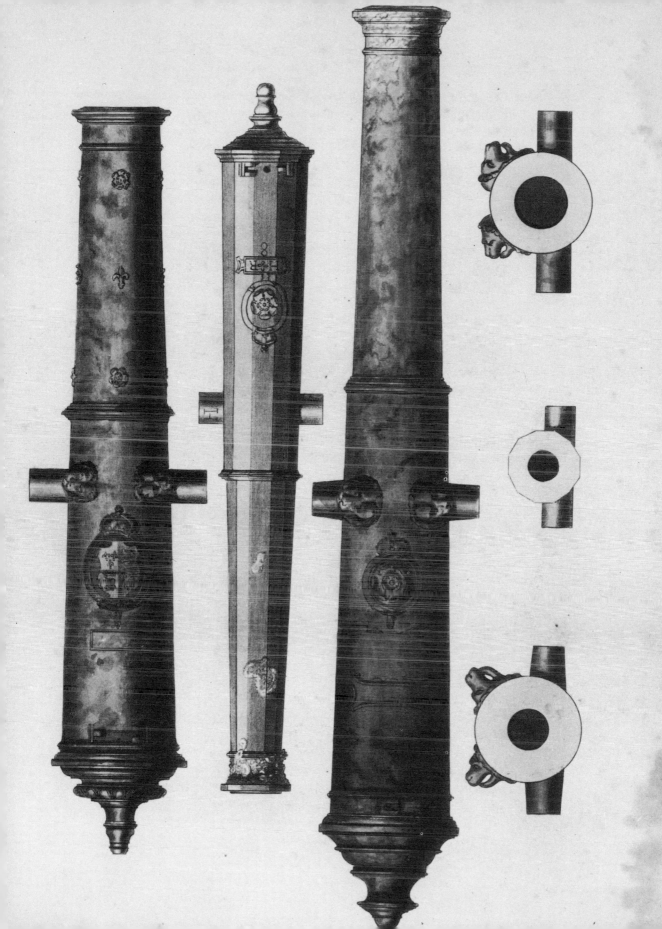

course of their diving, the Deanes were told by some local fishermen that their lines were always getting entangled with something on the seabed.

The Deanes were not only among the very first of the diving fraternity but they were also – as the new discipline required them to be – astute and perspicacious. Lines snag in timbers, fishermen fish in a place where they have found fish plentiful – and fish congregate in a place where they have found their own food plentiful. The logic is simple enough, but the consequences were to be complicated and far-reaching. At this time John Deane seems to have been working with a William Edwards, owner-skipper (one presumes) of the smack *Mary*, clearly the diving boat. In the place indicated by the fishermen were found lines that had become entangled in a baulk of timber, and these were duly freed. Following upon what was by now more than a hunch, the Deanes investigated further, and found more old timbers. There could be no doubt about it – they were definitely over a wreck.

On 16 June John Deane and Edwards reported finding a large cannon on the site. When landed and examined, the gun proved to be a bronze 32-pounder with a bore calibre of 6·4 inches. When it was cleaned some lettering on it became clear – and the lettering was a revelation. The inscription was in Latin – natural enough for the date of the cannon's manufacture, when Latin was still the international language. Translated, it read: "Henry VIII, King of England, France and Ireland, Invincible Defender of the Faith, made in 1542, by Arcanus de Arcanis." The latter was a well-known gunfounder of the sixteenth century.

Even more astonishing was the fact that the shot and the wad (which separated shot from charge) and the gunpowder itself were still in the gun. This ancient 32-pounder, then, had been ready for action when, mysteriously, it had gone to the bottom of the sea, along with this unknown vessel. The only great sea-change was that the iron shot had dwindled to nearly half its weight owing to its long contact with seawater. Moving on from this first exciting piece of salvage the Deanes discovered and managed to raise yet other guns, among them a massive cannon royal. This was a 68-pounder, of 8·54 calibre which, it was established, had also been made for Henry VIII although, interestingly enough, by British gunfounders, Robert and John Owyn Brothers, in 1535 – interestingly enough because Germany and Italy had been foremost in this field. It was clear that in Henry's reign technological advance at home had kept pace with the expensive expansion of the navy. This gun was also found to be ready for action, although again the shot had lost a great deal of weight due to its prolonged submersion.

The Board of Ordnance had of course been kept informed ever since the first discovery and it must now have been clear that the Deanes were diving

A copy of one of the certificates issued to authenticate objects salvaged by the Deane brothers and subsequently sold at auction.

RELICS FROM THE MARY ROSE

AT SPITHEAD,

Under Water 295 years.

WE the undersigned, DEANE and EDWARDS, do hereby CERTIFY that

purchased at our Public Sale, on the 12th November, 1840, at Portsmouth, (Mr. J. N. Robinson, Auctioneer,) the undermentioned lots of Wood and Relics recovered by us (under the authority of the Lords Commissioners of the Admiralty) in October 1840, from the Mary Rose, sunk in the REIGN of HENRY the EIGHTH, while forming the line of BATTLE with the ENGLISH FLEET, at SPITHEAD, in DEFENCE of PORTSMOUTH against the attack of a formidable FRENCH SQUADRON, in the Year 1545; by which event Sir George Carew, her Commander, and about 600 men suddenly perished.

on the remains of a Tudor warship, and one of considerable size. The wreck of the *Mary Rose* had long faded from even local memory, and so many wars and the intervening centuries had laid over the sunken ship a mist of forgetfulness almost as thick as the silt and sand that covered her timbers. For John Deane had already remarked that this ship only showed a foot in places above the surrounding seabed, whereas the *Royal George*, on which they had previously been diving, stood up proud – in places two gun-decks high – above her dark surround. The *Royal George* had sunk into an area of mud and clay, but this strange "new" wreck lay deep in silt.

Alexander McKee in *History Under the Sea* quotes:

Mr. Deane with spade, shovel, etc., then excavated a portion of the sand, etc., and fired a charge of gunpowder, and found on descending again that he had got into the hold of the unfortunate ship, having made a crater of large dimensions by this explosion. After this he made numerous descents at various times, and secured a variety of articles; a list of which Mr. Deane has kindly furnished. The greater portion of these singular articles were, by order of Mr. Deane, disposed of by public Auction . . .

A committee was established in London to investigate the origins of this mysterious ship. It cannot have been a great problem – even at the state of the art of historical research at that period in the nineteenth century. What Tudor warships were known to have sunk and where? The identification of the wreck, by means of the guns recovered from it, did not take very long, and by the autumn of the year 1836 the report of the committee had been accepted. It was agreed that there could be no doubt that "the Guns in question formed part of the Armament of the *Mary Rose* . . ." And so, as Robert Browning put it, "some lost lady of old years" was restored to memory. The *Mary Rose* came back into history.

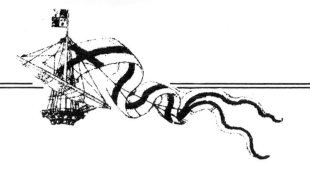

8. Lost – & Found Again

IT IS AN astonishing fact that the *Mary Rose*, having been found by the Deane brothers in the nineteenth century, yet again disappeared from view. After the initial excitement over the guns and other relics – including a comb among other simple human wants – the Solent waters resumed their drift and sway over the hull. Perhaps it was as well that the ship should be forgotten until the twentieth century when diving and archaeological techniques had improved to a degree that were undreamed of in previous years. In the days of the Deanes, those early pioneers, the objective had been to find guns (metal) and, if possible, precious metal and jewellery. The *Mary Rose* on first observation did not appear likely to yield much in the way of the latter: she was a ship-of-war setting out from her native Portsmouth for a battle-ground only a few miles away. It was unlikely that she would be carrying anything other than the immediate weapons of war and the basic requirements of living.

It remained for a remarkable man in the post-World War Two era (the era that one might well designate as that of Jacques-Ives Cousteau) to find once again this elusive sleeping warrior, cradled in her grave of sand and silt. I quote from Paul Johnstone in *The Archaeology of Ships*:

The device that completely changed the possibilities of this sort of operation [underwater archaeology] was evolved during the German

Alexander McKee, who found the site of the wreck of the Mary Rose and so opened the way for her excavation and recovery.

Opposite: At work on a recently raised gun.

Right: A diver on the seabed.

Left: One of the muzzle-loading guns on its wooden carriage photographed under water.

Below: Some of the guns recovered from the Mary Rose in the nineteenth century by the Deane brothers. Watercolours from James Deane's book, Cabinet of Submarine Recoveries, Relics and Antiquities. *These are wrought iron breech-loading guns mounted on gun beds.*

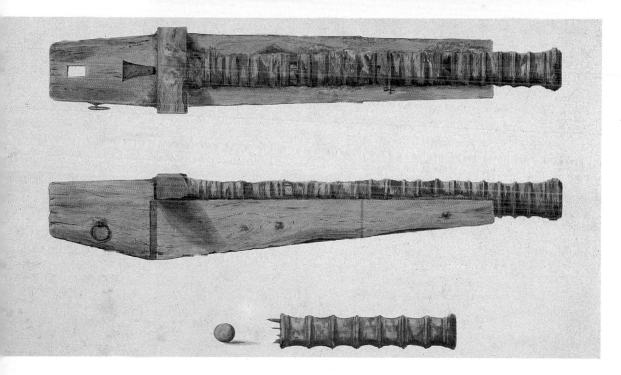

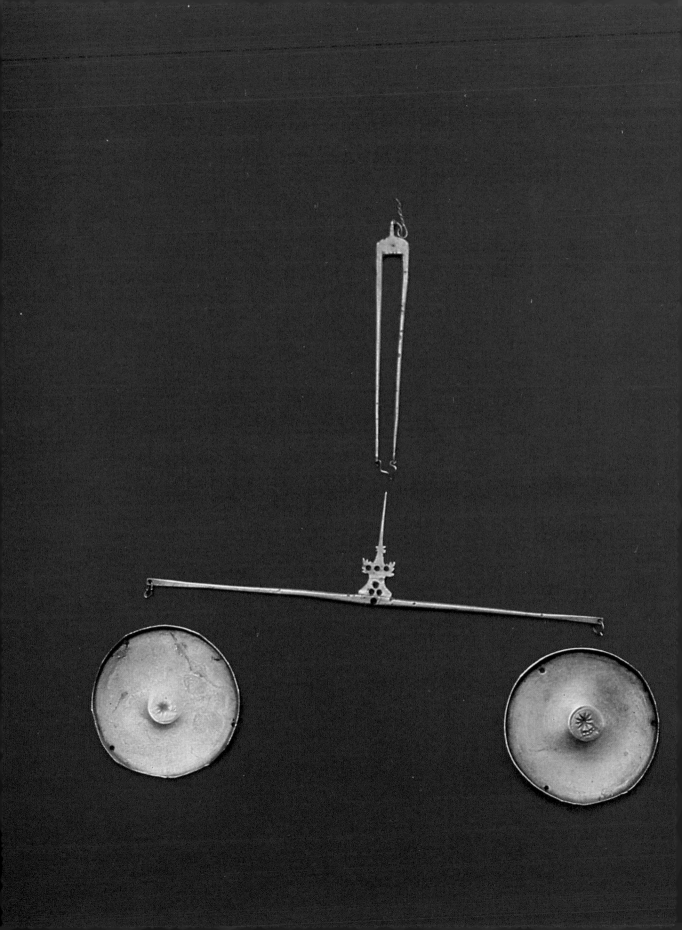

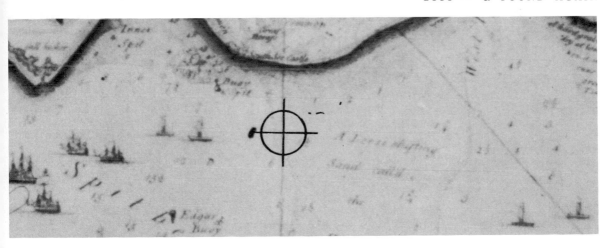

Above: The exact spot where the Mary Rose *lies.*

Opposite: Apothecaries' scales or balance: one of the loveliest of the items recovered to date.

occupation of France in the Second World War. A French naval officer, Jacques-Ives Cousteau, got an engineer, Emile Gagnan, to adapt for use with the Le Prieur diving apparatus an air-regulating device used in wartime wood burning gas-driven car engines. Thus was born the aqualung, the device which by freeing the diver from all the heavy and elaborate equipment of the hard-helmet era inspired the first great turning-point in archaeology underwater.

At first it was believed that only in clear waters like the Mediterranean and the Caribbean could the new technique be used successfully. These two seas were, at that time, clean and clear, and the beds of both of them were littered with underwater wrecks: in the Caribbean going back for several hundreds of years, and in the Mediterranean for well over two thousand. Unfortunately, in this early stage, very many mistakes were made, for this new liberty for man – the exploration of inner space – was a discipline that could not be comprehended quickly. As one of the Frenchmen who worked on an important wreck remarked at the time: "We have tried sincerely to the best of our ability . . . if we had been assisted in the beginning by an archaeologist, he would surely have noted with much greater accuracy the position of each object."

Alexander McKee was not only a keen aqualung diver but, fortunately for posterity, was trained in the disciplines of history, being both a military and aviation historian. He had then the requisite knowledge for a scientific approach to the matter of evidence as well as a good grasp of the deductive principle. His story of the rediscovery of the *Mary Rose* has been admirably told in his *King Henry VIII's Mary Rose*.

McKee had long suspected the earlier reports that the ship lay somewhere

Left: Mrs. Margaret Rule, who leads the team of archaeologists and volunteers who are excavating the Mary Rose.
Below: In the early days Alexander McKee and his team went out to the site of the Mary Rose in small boats like the fishing trawler Julie Anne, owned by Tony Glover.

near the wreck of the *Royal George*, for his analysis of the Battle of Portsmouth and the first accounts of her sinking suggested a position far from the *Royal George* and in comparatively shallow waters no great distance from Southsea Castle. Modern sonar confirmed this. The course of research led him and a fellow enthusiast, John Towse, to the Admiralty Hydrographic Department in London and to a survey of "Spithead with the Entrances to Portsmouth and Langstone Harbours" carried out in 1841 — near enough in time to the work of the Deanes for the position of the *Mary Rose* to have been still remembered.

The account takes on the exciting quality of a detective story as the two men unroll a large old chart, so large that they had to bend forward across the table on which they had it spread out in order to see the centre.

[It] took about ten seconds to unroll and then Towse and I leaned forward, taking in the red cross and name *Royal George* . . . then sliding down to the right to where we saw the red cross and the name *Edgar* [another known wreck] in 12–13 fathoms; and finally, almost automatically, going back to the *Royal George* and then looking up in the north-east arc towards the shallows of Spit Sand into our own search area. And there it was. A red cross and the name *Mary Rose*. In 6 fathoms. Towse gave an audible gasp . . . Fifteen seconds had now elapsed, from start to finish, from beginning to unroll the stiff canvas of the chart to making the astounding discovery. Then we began feverishly to transfer the *Mary Rose* position to our own charts, by our own separate methods, so that search could begin at once.

Both McKee and Towse knew that all wrecks in the Solent are marked by scour-pits. These are caused by the action of the current which, when it encounters an underwater object, causes an eddy — the speeded up water swirling on meeting the obstruction. The effect of this is that over the years, as the scour-pit develops, it is as if the wreck or whatever other large object may lie on the seabed seems to be digging itself steadily downwards. In fact, of course, it is the silt building up over it.

In the intervening years since the Deanes had remarked how only a few timbers of the *Mary Rose* projected a foot or so above the surround, she would have disappeared even further. By now, in the 1960s, like some giant dark mole, Henry VIII's ship would have burrowed out of sight. The double tides of the Solent, which some had thought would irrevocably destroy a wreck, in fact brought down in their sand and silt the very preservatives which would encapsulate a ship and keep her far better than the clear, tideless waters of the Mediterranean with their voracious teredo worm — and in recent years the even greater destruction caused by the thoughtless "bandit" aqualung divers. These were searching only for amphorae and anchors, and were quite untrained in archaeology and historical consideration. Ever since diving had first become a skill not too difficult to acquire, wrecks had been looted by people only interested in artefacts and totally unaware of how to preserve them once they had been brought ashore. Back into the sunlight and the oxygen that destroyed, came objects, particularly of iron, to be exhausted almost as swiftly as if they had been subjected to a blow-torch. Alexander McKee, who had done a considerable amount of skilled diving in the Mediterranean, had long considered that a Solent wreck might have survived better.

His opinion – that the *Mary Rose* was in fact protected in her deep sand burrow – was now reinforced by a skilled professional archaeologist, Margaret Rule, curator of the Roman Villa at Fishbourne, who had become fascinated by the new world of underwater archaeology since her first visit to Spithead when McKee and his helpers were working on the *Royal George*. She was to begin her initiation to the underwater world – like so many – with flippers and schnorkel, and was then to progress to aqualung, becoming one of the world's first women underwater archaeologists. She was to add to the original enthusiasts who had worked with McKee the disciplines of her profession, as well as those of one trained in the all-important techniques of conservation.

For McKee and his enthusiastic band of local helpers there was to be no great moment of discovery, when they *found* the *Mary Rose*. It was a very long business – like the growth of an oak tree – imposing upon this forgotten, sixteenth-century ship the new scrutiny of science. First of all, as McKee had long supposed, there was nothing showing above the surface where the Deanes had once dived. She had slipped even further into oblivion. By-products of Asdic gear (Sonar) then would be essential in order to detect – beneath the surface of the detritus into which she had sunk – the elemental skeleton of the ship.

The sleeping beauty was not simply found in her retreat and breathed upon: many devious methods of approach had first to be made in order to ensure that she lay there at all. Over the years since the 1960s many people and many organizations have lent a hand to find, excavate, and then restore this sunken warship; for it was seen from early days after Alexander McKee's first work upon the site that Henry VIII's great "carrack-style" fighting ship represented the bridge between the old and the new in the long history of warship design.

It was at this point that modern technology first met with the sixteenth century. A little over four hundred years separated them, and the new skills that were to reunite them were the ultimate result of that Renaissance in science and learning which had begun to waft into England from the

Above: In 1971 Alexander
McKee had a catamaran
Roger Grenville and an
inflatable rescue craft donated
by Avon as well the Julie
Anne to assist his
explorations.

continent during the reign of the man who had ordered the construction of
the *Mary Rose* – and had watched her wallow helplessly into the mud, sand
and water of the Solent.

Alexander McKee records how desolate were the diving conditions in his
early days. Visibility would often be under a foot as the divers worked on
excavating with hand or trowel on the site which, it had now been
established, contained something that was definitely not a part of the seabed.
Although a significant depression had already been detected by Alexander
McKee there was no sign of the hull, and no evidence save this and the
survey of 1841 giving the wreck's position. After initial probes had been
made, it was decided to bring modern science to bear. Side-scan sonar and a
profiler that could "read" below the mud were to indicate something
strange, an anomaly that lay below the mounds and indentations of the

surface. Both these modern techniques had been previously used for, among other things, geological surveys. Here in McKee's words is how the first scientific evidence confirmed his long-held view that the *Mary Rose* could be found and, if found, excavated. (It is significant that as early as 1941 in a Portsmouth paper McKee had written about the *Mary Rose*. Like the great Schliemann he had been dreaming of this day for many years.)

> What was to prove the most useful of the three scanner pictures was the first, taken from 200 feet ahead of the site. In effect, this was an almost instantaneous map of the anomaly, for the graph paper recorded its measurements, which were 200 feet long by 75 feet wide. This was larger than I expected the *Mary Rose* to be, but not at all excessive for a disturbance area which might contain much scattered wreckage . . . The alignment of the mound pattern appeared to be about south-east, very approximately, which was near enough to the heading of the *Mary Rose* and of the ''crested mound'' noted by Margot and I; and the Southsea ''transit'' went across the back end of the site – that is, it was the stern area, if she had sunk on her original heading.''

The buried ''W''-shaped anomaly found by modern science was in the very area shown on the nineteenth-century chart, the point where the red cross marked the last known position (established by the Deanes) of the *Mary Rose*. But as yet there was no firm evidence that this lump was indeed the Tudor ship, and now the real problems associated with the find started in earnest. As McKee had long foreseen, and Mrs Rule agreed with him, the position must at all costs be kept secret in view of the fact that Britain now bristled with aqualung divers – and McKee had seen in the Mediterranean what irresponsible divers could do to the wrecks of antiquity.

This might well be one of the most important wrecks in Northern Europe – a warship that had gone down very suddenly on a summer day in 1545. A whole Tudor world – explicit in a way that no books or records could ever be – might lie where the instruments tantalizingly suggested. If this was indeed so, then the *Mary Rose* would be a magnificent example of the kind of ''time capsule'' that archaeologists dream about. Undisturbed, save by the Deanes, for over four centuries the *Mary Rose* must somehow or other be preserved from vandals and foolish amateurs alike.

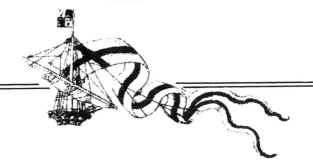

9. Salvation & Salvage

AT THAT TIME (1967) there was no legislation for the protection of wrecks on the ground of their historic value. Contracts to salvage ships (almost invariably modern ones) were sold to the highest bidder who would of course have previously assessed whether the wreck was capable of being raised or, more often, its scrap-value and its cargo. (A fascinating recent case of this kind of salvage has been the raising of the bullion from H.M.S. *Edinburgh* in the Barents Sea, lying in 800 foot of water.)

The Receiver of Wrecks, an official of H.M. Customs, kept the material when raised and put it up for auction after a year, the finder being recompensed by a percentage of the sale value. In the case of an ancient ship like the *Mary Rose* such a proceeding would have resulted in the disintegration of many, or most, of the artefacts – the iron guns, for instance, withering away under the exposure to oxygen. Both McKee and Mrs Rule were naturally eager to get the wreck site protected, but the Committee for Nautical Archaeology indicated that they were unable to help as matters stood; they had been campaigning for some time for a change in the law (so that underwater wreck sites could be protected in the same way as those on dry land). One of the great drawbacks was, of course, that the *Mary Rose* was not as yet really identified as a wreck. She was no more than a shadowy trace on a graph. It required almost an act of faith in modern technology – and in a nineteenth-century chart – to believe that the wreck of Henry VIII's great warship actually lay where a small band of enthusiasts believed it did.

Much discussion followed the events of that year and in November a Mary Rose (1967) Committee was formed in order to try and obtain some legal protection and "to find, excavate, raise and preserve for all time such remains of the ship *Mary Rose* as may be of historical and archaeological interest."

These were big, brave words at a time when no more than an "anomaly" had been discovered on the seabed. But, such was the faith of the *Mary Rose* believers, that the small Committee – consisting of Alexander McKee, Margaret Rule, Lt.-Cdr. Alan Bax R.N., and W. O. B. Majer (for the Society of Nautical Research) – soon had a letter under way to the Ministry of Defence. They suggested that the normal contract for salvage should be amended to provide for an archaeological investigation. It can be imagined that this was an unusual request to arrive in the corridors of Whitehall . . .

Contrary to popular belief that, in those "corridors of power", inertia always prevails, within three months the infant Committee was informed that they might apply for a lease of the seabed covering the area in which the Tudor warship lay (or was believed to lie). The leasing of the seabed had been not uncommon in the past to protect the interests of oyster-cultivators, but in recent years – with the exploration of the North Sea for oil and gas – a new vitality had been injected into this whole area of legislation. It appeared that Her Majesty the Queen (appropriately enough, in view of Henry VIII's connection with this stretch of sea) was the owner of the seabed at Spithead, and the Crown Estate Commissioners agreed to a lease of the *Mary Rose* site to this strange little Committee in Hampshire – for a peppercorn rent of £1 per annum.

"Armed," as the Mary Rose Trust booklet puts it, with "this rather flimsy legal protection, they began to organize the excavation and survey of the site." All this took great enthusiasm and courage, and it is an interesting fact that, throughout all the years since 1967, the project of this Tudor warship has aroused in all those connected with it a comradeship and burning enthusiasm that is rarely to be found in people except in times of war. Something far below the surface (about 60 foot at spring tides and 45 foot at neaps), something itself buried under about 20 foot of detritus – the sand, gravel and silt of centuries, together with the off-laden "gash" of all the ships that had passed that way – was accepting signals from another age, and, indeed, seemed almost to be signalling back itself.

The Herculean efforts made during the early stages to find concrete evidence of the ship can only be told (and have been) by McKee himself. ". . . I had planned mass digs by 22 divers using their hands only; indeed, during

October and November I had organized no fewer than six operations, five of which were cancelled by bad weather, and the sixth, the expensive one, proving abortive because of fog.'' The Portsmouth Fire Brigade were to play a considerable part in these early attempts at proving-excavations; for their hoses, directed underwater and not at burning houses, were to cut through the overlying silt that concealed the target. It took months of work, diving and trenching (with the water pumps), trenching and diving – and all the time there was the inevitable pressure of financing the project. The people engaged gave their services free – but boats and equipment and the power to operate equipment do not come free.

Throughout 1969 and 1970 the divers, aided by the Fire Brigade, continued whenever possible to improve their techniques, but success still eluded them. It says much, not only for their optimism, but for their steadfast endurance, that they still carried on while armchair experts ashore continued to maintain that it was all a wild goose chase and that the teams were working in the wrong place to start with. As always, those at all familiar with diving often cited Mediterranean examples of wrecks and continued to maintain that a ship sunk for over four hundred years in the turbid and tide-swept waters of the Solent would have long since disappeared. It was true that McKee, by carefully checking through all the early records, had shown that the Deanes in the early nineteenth cnetury had brought up guns and wood and a few artefacts from what was then said to have been the wreck of the *Mary Rose* – but was it really? And, in any case, no one knew for sure just where the Deanes had been diving – except that their real work had been on the *Royal George* and that wreck, as everyone knew, was a long way away from the position where these local enthusiasts were busying themselves.

After the disappointments of 1969 a new approach was decided on, and the *Mary Rose* Special Branch was formed, consisting of those people who were actively engaged on the Spithead project. Out of this came the offer of a really useful diving boat, with a good working area and even a sheltered cabin (something that these heroic volunteers had been without for years), at a special low rate from one of the members of the new Association. Something else that had been lacking in the past was now attended to – the laying of sound moorings at which the diving boat could secure while work was in progress. Much had been learned from the first days, but hard-won experience was now beginning to pay dividends.

At long last some wood appeared – a plank that, sadly enough, appeared to have been attacked by teredo worm, that scourge of wooden ships. Margaret Rule took charge of this first potential evidence of the ship, for conservation and analysis on the type and date of the wood. Fortunately it was soon found out that the worm which had attacked the wood had not been the deadly *teredo navalis* but a sort of second cousin: the initial fear that the ship might have been eaten to pieces was more or less dispelled. If the ship had been quickly covered by sediment, inimical to marine borers, and this plank remote from the wreck proper had been detached during the early attempts at salvage, or during the Deanes' work (or even torn away at some time by a dragging anchor), then there was still hope that the main body lay intact.

With the aid of an air-lift, something that the team had long been in need of but unable to finance, the first tangible evidence began to come to light. A large wooden cleat was recovered, proof in itself that the Tudor mariner was accustomed to making fast his ropes in exactly the same way as the modern sailor. Then came the great discovery, the one that was to clinch McKee's original deductions and to dispel the suspicions of the sceptics that there was nothing of interest in the area where so much work had been expended over the years. A sausage-shaped concretion (a compound of sand, shells, silicates and carbonates) was found where a team from the Royal Engineers, working with an air-lift the previous year, had reported a "contact".

McKee describes how this strange object was lifted aboard the diving vessel, and then: "Morrie later commented that I then went immediately into a state of shock . . . From the first moment I saw it in air, that grey concretion had a knobbly look – as if it concealed the multi-ringed barrel of a built-up gun."

The Deanes had raised guns of this type, which had deteriorated in the atmosphere – and no one then had known how to conserve such ancient metal lifted from the deep. People knew more now, and the gun (for such it was) was rushed to Southsea Castle for conservation. As the Mary Rose Trust 1981 publication records: "Superficially the gun seemed to be similar to the iron guns recovered by the Deanes, built-up of iron staves or bars formed into a cylinder and reinforced with collars and hoops. But examination by gamma radiography told a different story. The barrel was formed from a single plate of wrought iron, which had been formed into a cylindrical tube, with a single seam along its length."

This was a revelation. It was clear that a long, new look at the technology present in Tudor days was called for. To reinforce this barrel a series of hoops and collars had been hot-shrunk on to the tube. "The result was an efficient gas-tight cylinder, and it represents a separate and short-lived branch in the evolution of gun-making techniques." Chris O'Shea, a trained conservator, worked on the gun. It was found that the accretions and the blue-grey clay, which had blocked the muzzle, had preserved rather than annihilated this most unusual Tudor warship gun. Something else came to light – something that the Deanes had referred to after their accidental discovery of the *Mary Rose* and her armament. The gun was loaded. As

Right: An airlift is used to suck up unwanted spoil. The diver makes a thorough examinaton of the area using a small trowel or his hands alone.

O'Shea worked on the gun (a breech-loader) he came across the remnants of its charge, black powder, and then, beyond that, the wad of flax or hemp which separated it from the shot itself. The latter, unlike so many examples which were to emerge from other guns, was in perfect condition; the iron shot had been sealed in by the clay, into which the gun had dipped its muzzle at one end, while at the other it was sealed by the breech, the wad, and the gunpowder. This was a type of gun hitherto undiscovered, though it had indeed been known of from records as a "sling", the name for a long-range gun firing iron shot designed to penetrate an enemy's hull at some distance. Most guns of this period that had been recognized and classified were designed to fire stone shot or, in the case of the smaller guns, iron or lead pellets – like shrapnel. Here was a gun designed as a ship-destroyer, ancestor of so many that were – in the blood-stained history of sea warfare – to follow it over the centuries to come.

The discoveries of 1970 were to prove the turning point of this expedition under the sea, which had for so long soldiered on under a condition of hardship, poverty, and – in a sense – poor rations. Old pieces of wood (though fascinating to the specialist) have little glamour, but a gun really means something. Only gold doubloons, quintessence of every boy's *Treasure Island* days, could exceed the appeal of an ancient warship's gun. Now gifts and loans from private individuals as well as organizations began pouring in. "Nothing succeeds like success" – but success, too, has a price to pay.

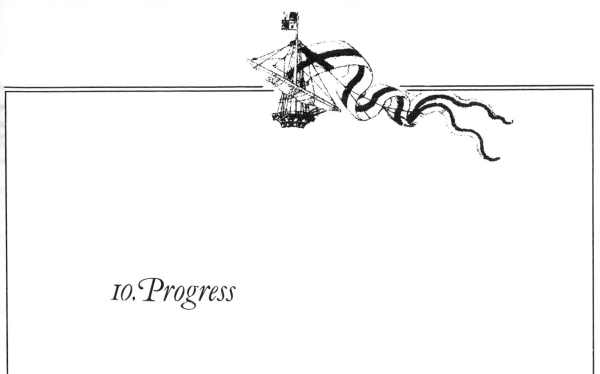

10. Progress

THERE COULD be no doubt by the end of the year 1971 that the Mary Rose team had indeed the *Mary Rose* of Henry VIII beneath them. The sceptics were silenced for ever more, and from all over the world – as the news became available – not only the enthusiasm of sub-aqua divers but the plaudits of underwater archaeologists cheered them on their way. The whole operation so far had in some ways resembled the pattern for the British during World War Two: the first hard, lonely years, with very limited resources and all the odds stacked against a small group of people; to be followed by evidence that their endurance was winning; and to be followed again by very great support as it was seen that they had proved their cause. The inflood of money and machinery and helpers was more than welcome.

Meanwhile, the archaeologist Margaret Rule had learned to dive. This was to be of permanent significance, for up to this time Mrs. Rule had been able to do little more than note the divers' findings, debrief them and make a record. A land archaeologist naturally found it difficult to envisage what lay down below and interpret accurately the reports of the divers, but a trained archaeologist who could also dive was an acquisition almost beyond price. Her determination to acquire this new skill was exceptionally praiseworthy since she was no longer a young woman, and diving with an aqualung is usually a "sport" taken up by people in youth. Her technical knowledge combined with this newly acquired ability was to go a long way towards getting the *Mary Rose* project substantially under way.

The *Mary Rose* booklet for 1981 has the following to say about these important early years:

Between 1971 and 1978 the base vessel was a lightly built catamaran, the *Roger Grenville*, named after the captain of the *Mary Rose* and donated by a local businessman. This provided a stable working platform for the small team of divers who worked on the site most weekends whenever tidal conditions and weather allowed. Early in 1971, a series of oak timbers were seen protruding from the seabed 100 metres to the south-west of where the gun had been found the previous year. Although the exposed tops of these timbers were eroded and worn by mechanical attrition and marine boring animals, the lower levels of the timbers, protected by the silt, were clean cut and hard and they shone with a warm red-brown glow in the light of the diving torch.

It was an exciting year. McKee's log book records:

As I came down on the wreck, it was almost dark and for the very first time I was very conscious of the hundreds of bodies lying literally only a few feet down among those timbers . . . A strange sensation, after all these years, clinging to the side of the *Mary Rose* with one hand, and digging down her side with the other. I had imagined the wreck many times, as it lay under the mud, while working out collapse stages, etc., but it was astonishing to see it so intact, solid proof of how wrong the sceptics can be!

In later years human bones were to become very familiar to the divers, as more and more of the ship was opened up by excavation. They came to mean fairly little – not so much that "familiarity breeds contempt" but because there were so many of them, as well as so many animal and fish bones, too, from the barrels that held the crew's provisions. The bones, like the ship itself, had been preserved by the all-invading silt and general detritus of the Solent. One diver remarked some years later in 1981: "Bones don't bother me. But, I must say, that a human skull has an impact." Another said, speaking of diving operations about the same time: "I was down there one day, working on a gun-carriage, and I found that I was not alone. Lying almost next to me was the skeleton of a man. He was still wearing his leather jacket and his leather shoes. Everything else had gone. But I found myself wondering: 'Who were you? Were you single or married? What kind of a life did you have? Were you happy or miserable – or were you, like most of us, a mixed-up muddle-up?' But then I had to get on with what I was doing."

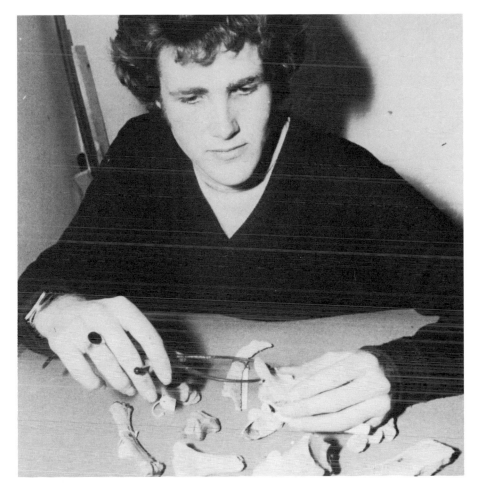

ob Stewart, one of the
rchaeological supervisors of
e Trust, has made a special
udy of life on board the
Mary Rose. *Here he examines*
me of the animal bones
covered from the wreck.

By 1973 the natural worry and concern of the *Mary Rose* Committee about
other people diving without scruples on the wreck was allayed. In that year,
and somewhat as a result of the activity about the wreck of Henry VIII's
warship, the "Protection of Wreck" Act was passed through Parliament.
This ensured that from henceforth an underwater "site" like that of the *Mary
Rose* could be preserved and secured just as well as an historic building or
any other place of archaeological interest above ground. One of the very first
ships to be protected under this Act was the *Mary Rose* — something that
would certainly have appealed to King Henry VIII who had a regal passion
for legislation. The Department of Trade henceforth licensed the *Mary Rose*
(1967) Committee to work on the site — to the exclusion of all others. For the
first time, since Alexander McKee and his members of the Southsea Branch of
the British Sub-Aqua Club had begun to dive on this almost forgotten "dent"

Three divers receive a briefing before beginning a dive.

in the seabed, the *Mary Rose* once again came under the protection of the Crown and the Commons. "Bluff King Hal" would have been delighted.

Gradually over the years the hull was revealed. It was a very difficult business for the divers and far from romantic, as McKee's account (*King Henry VIII's Mary Rose*) reveals:

> Inboard, cautious excavation by hand at selected points in a narrow trench flanking the inner side-planking had to be stopped time after time, just when it was getting interesting, because the uncovered wreckage was too complicated and fragile to leave uncovered . . .

There were other problems:

> Dave Felton had the initial task of removing this compacted fill . . . what came to the surface was a great mass of interlocked laminaria weed and roots, together with a large expanse of untreated sewage, the stench from which nearly made us all sick. A large conger eel, which had apparently been living in the outboard excavation, and loving it, shot past Felton's face, narrowly escaping going up the air-lift with the effluent . . . on another occasion the scene was further polluted, apparently by an upstream oil-tanker, and the air-lifters had first to plunge through surface water contaminated by several inches of reeking crude oil before descending to the sewage-impregnated seaweed.

In these comparatively early years of the excavation of the *Mary Rose* it was concluded from the very beginning that the inside of the hull should be left untouched until the outside had been thoroughly investigated, and until it had been established in what direction the ship was lying. According to what was known about the Battle of Portsmouth the vessel should have been heading southerly, away from the land and the harbour. But it was fairly soon established that the bows of the *Mary Rose* were pointed towards the north. This was very difficult to explain. Either the French claim that she had been hit by their gunfire was true, or the ship had turned about during her descent through the water. There is no evidence either way, although the accounts of the action would surely tell if the *Mary Rose* had been damaged and forced to turn back. Subsequent investigations when the hull is completely examined may reveal the truth of the matter.

Somewhat analogous to the story of the *Mary Rose* is that of the Swedish warship *Wasa*, although the latter was a completely new vessel and had never seen any action. On 10 August 1628 while on her maiden voyage she was struck by a squall, heeled over, dipped her gunports under water and went straight to the bottom. The salient difference between the two ships was that the *Wasa* sank in the Baltic where the relatively fresh water means that the

shipworm cannot live. As Paul Johnstone tells the story in *The Archaeology of Ships*: "By 1958 a specially formed committee had reported that it was feasible to salvage the *Wasa* and that the attempt should go ahead." The ship had first of all to be moved into shallower water for she was lying in about 110 feet (33.5 metres). In this respect McKee and the *Mary Rose* team were lucky in that Henry VIII's warship lay at a depth where, despite the tides and currents of the area, she was comparatively easy to get at. The *Wasa* was indeed successfully moved into 50 feet (15 metres) – something like the depth at which the *Mary Rose* lies – and from there – by the use of pontoons and hydraulic jacks – she was brought back again into the light and the astonished gaze of many thousands of Swedes whose distant ancestors had seen her fateful sinking. Older ships than the *Wasa* had been found, but she was the first specifically named ship, whose brief history was known, ever to

A diver leaves the base vessel Sleipner *under the watchful eye of archaeological supervisor Chris Dobbs.*

be recovered. She rests now in the *Wasa* Museum, a source of historic interest and delight to her countrymen and to countless thousands of tourists.

It was always the dream of the *Mary Rose* team that something similar to the operation could be carried out on her. True, she was a much older ship than the *Wasa*, but this very fact produced all the more challenge. The Tudor warship marked a great transitional point in the construction of warships – the moment when the heavy gun designed to fire broadsides first appeared upon the waters. Just as the *Wasa* had revealed to historians and archaeologists not only the splendour of seventeenth-century Swedish woodcarving but many items of everyday life aboard ship, so the *Mary Rose* should contain a whole picture of an earlier world wrapped within her frame.

No archaeological land-site is ever likely to be as perfect as a ship which has sunk at a given moment and place, with all her life intact about her, and with only the ordinary detritus of subsequent centuries lying above her. Cities and palaces get changed, get built upon, get ransacked, get forgotten as the houses and villages of later men spring up on the same site; but a ship encapsulated in the ocean, preserved by her lonely environment, suffers little. The worst that can happen – as in the case of so many Mediterranean wrecks – is the onslaught of a deadly shipworm like the *Teredo Navalis*. But this enemy of wooden structures does not take kindly to the colder waters of the North and the *Mary Rose* team had good reason to hope that the structure of their ship was sound.

The greatest experts at this time on the conservation and preservation of an old wooden warship were, of course, the staff of the Stockholm Museum which held the *Wasa*. Early in 1972 the Director visited Portsmouth and placed at the disposal of the *Mary Rose* team the knowledge and experience (often painfully gained) of his experts. The *Mary Rose* was no longer a dream sustained by a small group of Portsmouth eccentrics, but was fast becoming an international source of permanent interest.

II. Formation of the Trust

THE AIM ALL along had been not only to find the *Mary Rose* (this had now been done), not only to make as thorough an investigation as possible of her hull, not only to bring up to the surface whatever weapons and other artefacts that might be found: over and above all was an ultimate aim – to raise the ship herself, as had been done with the *Wasa*. Now, as developments proceeded over the years, it was clear that what Alexander McKee called a project "begun with five men and a boat" had become of international status and had acquired a momentum of its own. There could be no turning back from the larger implications of the lifting and conservation of objects found in and around the ship (an expensive process in itself), but the ultimate aim of raising and transferring her to a special museum where her timbers could be treated and preserved was a task that in itself might take many years.

The Swedes could as yet see no end to the task of keeping the *Wasa* in a "watery condition" that would prevent those old timbers, long-saturated with salt water, from drying out and splitting. It was clear enough that the *Mary Rose* might present an even bigger problem.

By the beginning of the seventeenth century, the exposed superstructure [of the *Mary Rose*] had been eroded and weakened by mechanical attrition and biological degradation. Gunports fell from their corroded hinges and the outer planking of the ship collapsed into the scour pit to be followed shortly after by the frames or ribs of the upper part of the hull. Once the superstructure had collapsed into the scour pit, the scouring action of the currents were substantially reduced and the site rapidly stabilised . . . The underside of the ship lies deep in the mud and present evidence suggests that this side of the ship was never exposed to excessive current action and that it is well preserved to a height of some 13 metres above the keel. (Mary Rose Trust, 1981)

Whereas the *Wasa* had settled in a more or less upright position, the *Mary Rose* was lying well over to starboard while her port side had been heavily eroded to below her original water line. The obscuring and healing silts appeared to have preserved the starboard side from erosion almost intact. The two ships, then, were far from identical – in that the older ship, the *Mary Rose*, was lying at an awkward angle and did not appear to be as "entire" as the *Wasa*. This in itself did not matter so much, since no one can hope to "float" an old sunken ship to the surface on the basis that it will hold the water on its own. In any and every case, what the would-be salvage operator is faced with is the problem of lifting a heavy, inert weight to the surface – a dead weight, in the old phrase, which must be brought aloft – without its timbers and their fastenings collapsing under the change from the relative weightlessness of underwater to the immediate weight conditions of being up in the open air. (A fat man can float easily in the sea – and dive beneath it – but once he comes back to the land will notice a great deal of difference . . .)

From 1965 to 1978 the dedicated team working on the *Mary Rose* had laid the foundations upon which all the future work could be based. At the close of these thirteen years they had also made a breakthrough by excavating a major trench across the bows of the ship. The main deck and the orlop deck (the lowest in a warship) had been revealed for examination. The belongings of soldiers and sailors were found scattered across the main deck, where they had doubtless fallen at the moment that the ship heeled and went to the bottom.

As the years went by, more and more evidence of the Tudor world was uncovered, giving a picture of those days in intimate detail. In the past, historians writing about the period have had to be content with what could be found out from letters, books, documents, and a careful study of portraits. But, almost inevitably, those who were painted and those who wrote letters or documents came very largely from one class: comparatively little was known about "the short and simple annals of the poor". As the archaeologists and the divers uncovered more and more of the social and private history revealed by the objects within the hull of the *Mary Rose* a new world opened up.

It is a world of astonishing fascination – for this fascination resides not only in the artefacts themselves but in the knowledge that these unknown and nameless men were our ancestors. Contemplating an archer's bow of yew, a sailmaker's thimble, or a shawm (that forerunner of the oboe, and one of the very few ever found in Europe) is something that brings back a vivid picture of a world that was once as instinct with life as the one we know ourselves. Admiration at the craft of the turner in those days, of the gunfounder, or the leather-worker, is not untinged with melancholy:

> For them no more the blazing hearth shall burn,
> Or busy housewife ply her evening care;
> No children run to lisp their sire's return,
> Or climb his knees the envied kiss to share.
>
> (Thomas Gray)

1978 was a crucial year in the history of the reborn *Mary Rose*. The discoverers, and those who had first lent their sparetime work to the weekend diving and the bringing of fragments of the wreck and her contents to the surface, would no longer be able to cope with the demands that were now to be made upon them. (Not to be too fanciful, it was as if the Tudor warship was struggling to be free, and make her statement to an alien century.) A massive effort was required, involving large-scale organization and fund-raising on a national and international basis.

The *Mary Rose* Committee convened two meetings in Portsmouth to examine the implications of all the new discoveries, embodying their hard-earned information about the state of the hull and its fittings, the objects they had recovered, and the certain likelihood of the kind of artefacts and nautical gear that would be found in the deeper layers of the ship. Naval architects, archaeologists and ship historians considered the evidence, and came to the conclusion that the remains of the ship were of sufficient value to nautical science, as well as to the general public who would visit a suitably prepared museum, that the *Mary Rose* should be totally excavated. Everything found should then be carefully conserved and a museum should be found – or newly built – for their display. The second gathering of experts consisted of those who dealt in the real practicality of *how* such could be done – particularly the raising of the hull. Theirs was a harder task for, while it was comparatively easy to say how great an addition to knowledge it would be to bring up all this new evidence, it was far more difficult to say how the hull itself could best be raised – if raised at all. However, the evidence

Lieutenant-Commander Peter Whitlock MBE RN (retired), Historian to the Mary Rose *project, discusses one of the pulley blocks from the* Mary Rose *with Sue Green, a staff member.*

available from the Swedish *Wasa* (as well as all the new information pouring in from the deep sea work in the North Sea) had by now convinced the members of this world of high skilled underwater technologists that a lift was feasible.

It was decided to form the *Mary Rose* Trust. This was an inevitable but distant move from the small Committee of 1967, where the main aim had been

Richard Harrison, Executive Director of the Mary Rose *Trust.*

no more than to ensure that the warship was protected from the depredations of underwater vandals. (The protection of the site from other ships, or yachts even, carelessly anchoring above or discharging their garbage on to the site, had long been undertaken by the Royal Navy.)

The objectives of the *Mary Rose* Trust were declared to be – as they remain today – much the same as the basic ones that Alexander McKee had earlier outlined:

> To find, record, excavate, raise, bring ashore, preserve, publish, report on and display for all time in Portsmouth the *Mary Rose*. [Secondly] To establish, equip and maintain a museum, or museums in Portsmouth to house the *Mary Rose* and related or associated material. [Thirdly] To promote and develop interest, research and knowledge relating to the *Mary Rose* and all matters relating to, or associated with her, and all matters relating to underwater cultural heritage. All for the education and benefit of the nation.

With the inauguration of the Trust in January 1979 it was clear enough that industry and business, the nautical world both nationally and internationally, and archaeologists everywhere (not forgetting the general public itself) were enthusiastically aroused by the idea of raising from the seabed this Tudor warship that had sunk in 1545. At the first meeting of the Trust Sir Eric Drake CBE was elected Chairman, and at the same time it was announced that His Royal Highness Prince Charles had agreed to be the first President. Prince Charles, himself a sailor as well as a former naval officer, a keen aqualung diver (he was later to dive on the ship on several occasions), was the most suitable President that there could ever have been. The *Mary Rose* came under royal patronage for the first time in all those centuries since King Henry VIII had dined aboard her.

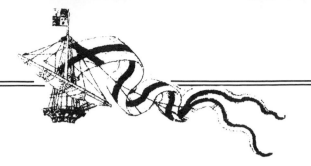

12. Two Worlds Meet

BENJAMIN DISRAELI in one of his early books described the British as being "two nations". He was referring to the immense divide in the nineteenth century between the rich and the poor. Such, of course, was almost as true in the reign of Henry VIII, when those born to wealth and high estate were very distinct from the soldiers and sailors who served them aboard a ship such as the *Mary Rose*. At the same time, since they lived together so closely and roughly, there was none of that sense of class distinction that prevailed in Victorian times. On the other hand, divisions of rank there have always been aboard ship; for instance, a miniature silver bosun's call that was later to emerge from the *Mary Rose* was clearly a badge of rank. (It is in marked contrast with yet another, full-sized, bosun's call which has been found, and which would not seem unfamiliar in the twentieth-century Navy.) The *Mary Rose* was a warship of (for that time) great size. The captain would have been the captain. The carpenter (always an important man aboard any ship), the sailmaker, the gunners, the archers (far from an obsolete profession for many years), all would have discharged their separate inter-related functions.

Compared with the French, though, and indeed most people on the continent, the English ate well. The Rev. William Harrison, writing some thirty years after the death of the *Mary Rose*, but describing the same world, commented: "The bread throughout our land is made of such grain as the soil yieldeth, nevertheless the gentility commonly provide themselves sufficiently of wheat for their own tables, while their household and poor neighbours in some shires are forced to content themselves with rye or barley . . .'' Aboard the *Mary Rose* the bread was probably of wheat or rye, or a mixture, for both were grown extensively in the south of England and as an Elizabethan traveller observed: "The Englishman eat barley and rye brown bread, and prefer it to white bread as abiding longer in the stomach . . .'' He adds that the country yields "all kinds of corn in plenty''.

Many fish bones found on the site have shown, as might indeed be expected in a ship leaving a Channel port, that fish formed a staple part of the diet.

But meat and bread were the principal foods, for vegetables were little accounted (the potato of course had not yet arrived from America) and cabbage and peas formed the main crops from the country round about. The amount of meat that the English ate always amazed foreign visitors – and was to continue to do so for centuries. In the later excavation of the *Mary Rose* barrels of animal bones – beef, pork, mutton – have confirmed that this was indeed so.

The *Mary Rose*, as she began to reveal in the years from 1979 onwards, was a living book of the Tudor period, proving the accounts of some early travellers and writers and disproving the suppositions of some later historians. The great historian G. M. Trevelyan, for instance, was proved abundantly right in his statement that "the southern English walked on leather, and disdained the 'wooden shoes' that foreigners were fain to wear''. A large number of leather shoes have been found, the soles made from cow- or ox-hide, the uppers of sheepskin. In Europe, as in the north of England, clogs were the standard footwear.

The most important moment in the second life of the *Mary Rose* began with Alexander McKee's discovery of her in the 1960s. The second most important was the formation of the Trust in 1979. In that year the first overall view of the objects and the commitments of the Trust were most carefully examined – in a twentieth-century manner. This was where the sixteenth-century world met its successor.

The facts about the *Mary Rose*, as known at that time and before further investigations were completed, need to be summarized. Built at Portsmouth in 1509–10, she underwent a complete rebuild in 1536. Unlike the *Wasa* she was not new to action, and had been described by Sir Edward Howard in 1513 as "the flower I trow of all ships that ever sailed''. This was just after she had been on sea trials in an earlier campaign against the French. It is worth noting that at that time in her life her complement had consisted of 120 mariners, 251 soldiers, 20 gunners, five trumpeters and 36

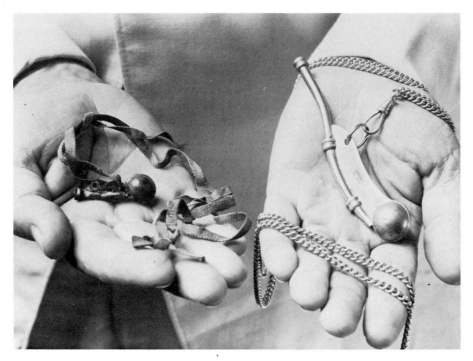

servants. When she sank in July 1545 she had about 700 men aboard her; even with a normal complement of 415, this was vastly in excess of requirements and was probably made up of archers and foot soldiers. The ratio of gunners to mariners would have greatly altered since her conversion to an "all gun" ship in 1536. Her armament at the time would appear to have been 91 guns, some of bronze and others of iron. The main hull, after her rebuilding, was carvel-planked and was fixed with treenails of wood. Unfortunately, many of the other interior parts of the ship were iron fastened: the nails of course have wasted away through chemical action and the effect of this deterioration has caused grave problems for the archaeologists and recovery team. (The *Wasa* suffered even more, being iron fastened throughout, and the Swedish team had to refasten her with steel before she could be lifted.)

The exact dimensions of the *Mary Rose* cannot be completely confirmed until she has been raised, but they would appear to be about 175 feet in overall length and with a keel length of some 130 feet. (She had large overhangs due to the fore- and after-castles, those relics of earlier days which would gradually wane away in the years to come.) She lies on the edge of Spitsands, $1\frac{1}{2}$ miles from the entrance to Portsmouth Harbour (longitude 01° 06′ West, latitude 50° 45′ 48″ North). She is shallow-sunk at about 35

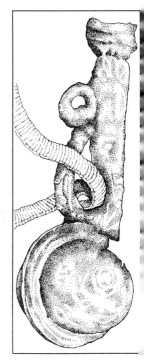

feet at neap-tides. Slightly down by the stern and heeled to starboard at
about 60°, she was until recently covered by mud and sediment – protected
would be the better word. The risk she now stands before she is raised is
from water action, gribble worm and, unfortunately, perhaps the *teredo
navalis*. The latter, rarely found in northern waters in earlier centuries even
though it came back in the hulls of wooden ships from other warmer seas, has
been given a new lease of life in certain areas. Where the *teredo navalis*, being
a southerner, would have died from cold in other days it sometimes now
survives because of the massive warm effluent pouring out from commercial
areas and ports.

In 1979, the first year of the Trust, it was adjudged that the principal
action was to remove from the buried hull all the secondary sediments which
concealed it. Once this was done the next objective would be to remove the
primary sediments that had permeated the *Mary Rose* soon after she sank.
"Excavation in 1979 and 1980 showed that a substantial portion of three
decks survive in the waist of the ship and a part of the fourth deck and
indications of a fifth have been found in the sterncastle. The hold is low with
only 5 feet 9 inches of headroom and apart from a few barrels and a store of
logs for the galley it seems to have been filled with flint ballast" (Mary Rose
Trust 1981).

It is interesting to note that a type of silver birch found only in Scotland
formed part of the firewood for the galley. In the year previous to her
sinking, the *Mary Rose* had been up in Scottish waters, keeping a watch and
ward over the north where pro-French sympathizers (exacerbated by Henry
VIII's policies) were flourishing. In well-wooded Hampshire there was no
shortage of fuel, but these birch logs must certainly have come from
Scotland.

Don Bullivant, a diver who has worked on the *Mary Rose* since 1965, was
one of those who helped to excavate the galley area. He described how he
first came across the rim of the vast copper pot probably used for cooking.
(Sailors then, as even now in some ships, depended upon a large general
stock-pot.) He describes how uneasy he felt as the general size and shape
began to emerge, for it bore every resemblance to a World War Two mine.
(The writer was in Portsmouth during some of the heavy bombing and
mining of the port and its approaches and can well understand his
apprehension . . .)

In October 1979 a major step forward was made by the Trust when it
acquired a proper base for all its activities – from office work to conservation
and preservation – in The Old Bond Store in Warblington Street, Old
Portsmouth. Prior to this the various workers had occupied a number of
temporary "homes", but they now had a secure operational headquarters

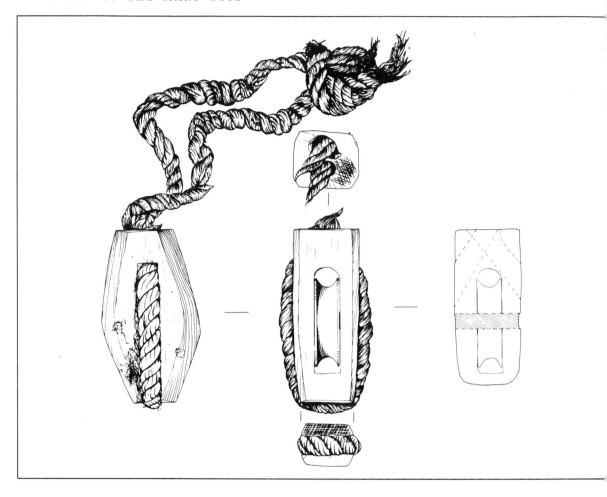

made available to them by Whitbread Wessex. Throughout the winter of 1979–80 work was carried out so as to provide accommodation for finds as they came ashore, storage, a drawing office, a photographic studio, and a suitable area for the treatment and conservation of the finds.

The great event of 1979, which went far towards making all the subsequent work upon the *Mary Rose* a possibility for a considerable team of divers (volunteers coming from not only England but the continent and America), was the acquisition of the *Sleipner*. Originally an Admiralty lifting craft of 370 tons, she had been later acquired by Sweden and had been one of the vessels used in the raising of the *Wasa*. After a considerable amount of conversion work, to fit her for her new task of lying moored in the immediate vicinity of the *Mary Rose*, she was towed out to the site, providing, in subsequent years, an efficient working platform for the divers and the on-

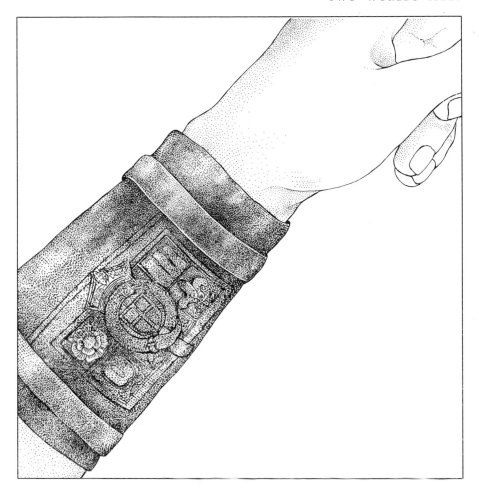

Left: A drawing of wooden
pulley blocks with some of the
original rope still intact which
were found in the wreck of the
Mary Rose.
Right: One of the leather
wrist guards worn by the
archers on board the Mary
Rose.

site archaeological team under Mrs. Margaret Rule. Here the objects found
are brought aboard, ranging from large cannons to small delicate pieces like
pocket sundials, compasses, and the personal possessions of the crew. After
an initial hosing down and cleaning off they are then taken ashore, and
transported to Warblington Street, for assessment, documenting and subsequent conservation.

During this first year with the *Sleipner* in position, and with the
Warblington Street base in full operation, major results were achieved,
despite the fact that the visibility on a good day was no more than 12 to 18
feet. (It can be judged what the visibility over the wreck was on a bad day,
common enough in the area.) At this point the advantages available to the
Mary Rose Trust, due to financial improvement and the increasing publicity
that the venture was receiving from press, radio and television, became

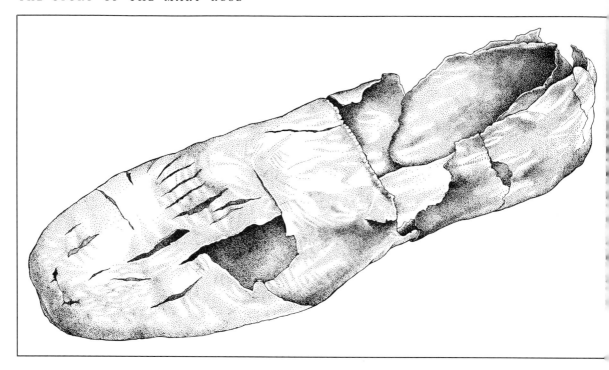

A drawing of a leather shoe from the Mary Rose.

apparent. Low light intensity underwater video cameras, with a wide angle lens, giving an advantage over the human eye of about ten per cent, enabled those directing from aboard the *Sleipner* to assess and interpret for the benefit of those working below just what it was that they were uncovering. With the aid of their modern equipment and the stable base of the diving ship above them, the divers were getting steadily deeper into the *Mary Rose* and the finds for the year 1979 began to come to the surface in ever-increasing numbers.

Excellent and strong rigging blocks, some with the rope strop built into the shell, showed the mastery of their craft by the Tudor blockmaker and rigger. Gold coins known as "angels", worth six shillings and eight pence when minted (a day's pay for a Vice-Admiral and about a month's for a gunner of the time), and leather shoes (some with the foot bones still inside them) were further aspects of this buried world that twentieth-century men with the aid of twentieth-century scientific technology were bringing back into the light. Six foot long-bows of yew were a reminder of the terrible English archer, who had been the scourge of France on many a famous battlefield. Then a large, bronze muzzle-loading gun, complete upon its wooden carriage, spoke of the new age in warfare – no longer only in the siege of fortified towns and castles, but upon the oceans of the world.

Opposite: Examining, repairing and conserving leather. Daphne Smith at work, with a leather jerkin.

120

Far left: This beautiful plaque of two angels in high relief on bone or possibly ivory was probably a decoration for the spine of a book.

Near left: Many angel coins have been recovered.

Below: A double-gimballed compass in its original box.

Above right: From the barber surgeon's collection: Bowls and jars including a bleeding bowl, chafing dish and drug flask. The syringe is made of pewter; another syringe of bronze alloy has also been found.

Below right: A wooden gaming board with a wind musical instrument, a leather purse, a book cover, three trading tokens, two dice, a gaming counter and the spur of a fighting cock.

Above: The pocket sun-dial, the Tudor equivalent of a wrist watch. Made of box-wood it is shown with the lid removed.

Left: A wooden comb with its leather case, a wooden pomander and a bone manicure set. With chain: a hanger for securing a purse or pouch to a belt.

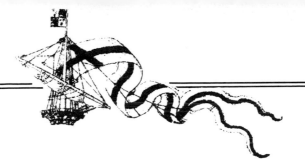

13. Gunners, Archers & Others

THE ARMAMENT of the *Mary Rose*, and the ships which were to follow her, made a great demand, an inroad indeed, upon an island like England – well-wooded and furnished with metals though it was. Coal, copper, iron, lead and tin were all being heavily mined in the reign of King Henry VIII, and these provided the essentials for gun-founding and, thus, for gunnery warfare. Some fifty years after she sank the House of Commons heard a eulogy of the country's resources: "Our iron appeareth to be a particular blessing of God given only to England, for the defence thereof, for albeit most countries have their iron, yet none of them all have iron of that toughness and validity to make such ordnance of"

To smelt the metals required for this new age of the broadside and its cannons, great forests were slowly being cut down – as indeed they were for the ships themselves. Yet it was still a long time before, in the age of Nelson, the country became very largely dependent upon Baltic oak. The oak, the elm and other woods that went into the *Mary Rose* were all home-grown. Similarly, the gunpowder – until many years later the English expanded into the East – was compounded of charcoal, saltpetre and sulphur from the island.

Most of the guns aboard the *Mary Rose* were of iron, although 15 out of her 91 are recorded in the Antony Roll as having been of brass. The very names

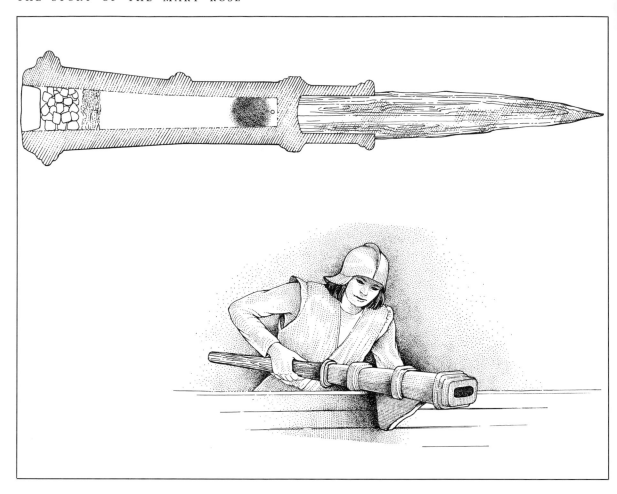

of these early pieces of ordnance have a certain sinister poetry of their own. Of brass there were cannons, demi-cannons, culverins, demi-culverins, sakers, and falcons. Of iron there were port pieces, slings, demi-slings, quarter-slings, fowlers, bases, top pieces, hailshot pieces, and hand guns. The loosely-used term ''brass'' guns implied that the composition was about 100 parts copper to ten parts of copper and zinc and eight parts tin. The brass guns cost about three times as much as the iron guns to manufacture.

Although the breech-loading gun, as has been seen from pieces aboard the *Mary Rose*, was well established, the difficulties and dangers encountered with breech-loading meant that for many centuries its place was taken by the, apparently, more simple muzzle-loader. Muzzle-loading, however, was an awkward and clumsy business, as gunners were to realize well into the nineteenth century, but the dangers of breech-loading – especially aboard a

Above: How the breech-loading guns worked.
Left: A small muzzle-loading anti-personnel gun found on the Mary Rose *still loaded with hail shot, wad and powder. A wooden tiller or butt was inserted in the end of the gun which could be hooked over the side of the ship or a rail by means of a flange projecting from the underside of the barrel.*

ship – outweighed its obvious advantages. To hold the breech successfully against the pressure of the explosion was never really solved until, many centuries after the *Mary Rose*, the interrupted thread was chanced upon. (The thread in the breech block and the thread in the barrel had regular gaps, so that when the block was swung to and given a swift turn, both parts were "married", and united like a solid piece of metal.)

One of the most interesting types of gun recovered so far from the *Mary Rose* is the anti-personnel, hailshot weapon. These had a rectangular bore and were muzzle-loaders, the iron barrels having been cast in a mould (as can be seen by the fact that the 'flashing' caused by the flow of the metal through the joints of the mould can be clearly discerned). The inventory of the ship's armament shows that she carried 20 of these pieces – something that would have made a formidable hail of fire when closing an enemy or, alternatively,

127

Left: A splendid lion's head from one of the bronze muzzle-loading guns.

in repelling boarders. The irregular-shaped iron "dice" of the shot were still in the guns, together with the wad and the gunpowder charge. These guns were easily portable, and had beneath them a projecting piece of iron which could be used to hook them over any convenient rail to steady them while the gunner took aim, as well as to withstand the shock of the recoil. At the rear of the gun a socket had been left in the casting into which a wooden stock or tiller was inserted so that when the gun was hooked in place, the gunner could direct the piece on to his required line of fire.

Some idea of the amount of work involved in the new progress and of the results achieved by it can be gauged by this report for 1980 compiled by Peter Whitlock on behalf of the *Mary Rose* Trust. After noting that, because of financial considerations that year, operational work was curtailed to a season lasting only from May to August, he goes on to show just how much in that comparatively brief season was achieved and in what direction:

The team of six full time diving archaeologists under the direction of Mrs. Margaret Rule . . . staunchly supported by volunteer divers from many parts of the world, ran a daily programme from dawn to dusk. 7,025 dives were made with 4,218 man hours on and below the seabed, up to 60 feet from the surface. The ship lies on a north/south line, bows north, resting

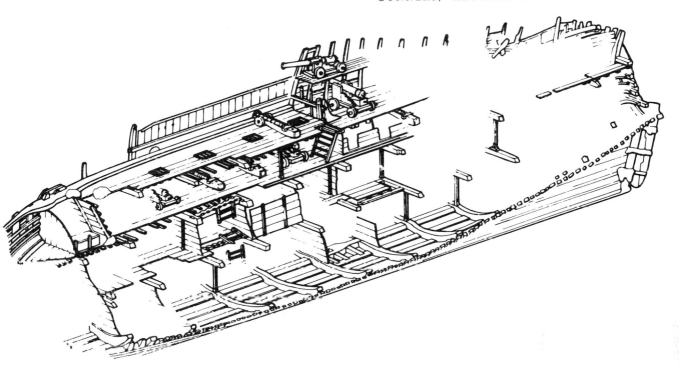

Above: The Mary Rose *structures as revealed in October 1980.*

on her starboard side at an angle of 60°. Most of the clinker-built high castle structures have been eroded away, likewise a large part of the port side of the hull, but the rest of the ship is preserved to a remarkably high degree. Frames, riders, and deck beams are in place – the upper deck surviving to a breadth of nine feet in the waist of the ship, the main and orlop deck are even more promising. [The orlop was a plank platform laid over the beams in the hold, on which the cables were usually coiled and various store-rooms were sited.] The wrought iron fastenings of the deck planking have corroded away; therefore planking is only held in place by angle of slope, snugness of fit, and surrounding silt.

What this meant was that all this planking had to be removed along with the associated structure. This of course entailed much extra work, but it was necessary for the safety of divers and its removal also meant that artefacts contained in the ship could be got at more easily. The alternative was to refix deck planking and supporting structure, replacing the eroded wrought iron fastenings. The intention is that when the ship is raised all the timbers so moved will be replaced in their original positions. The report continues:

The main deck still carries several guns of bronze and iron in position on their carriages . . . The work in 1980 was concentrated on excavation of

129

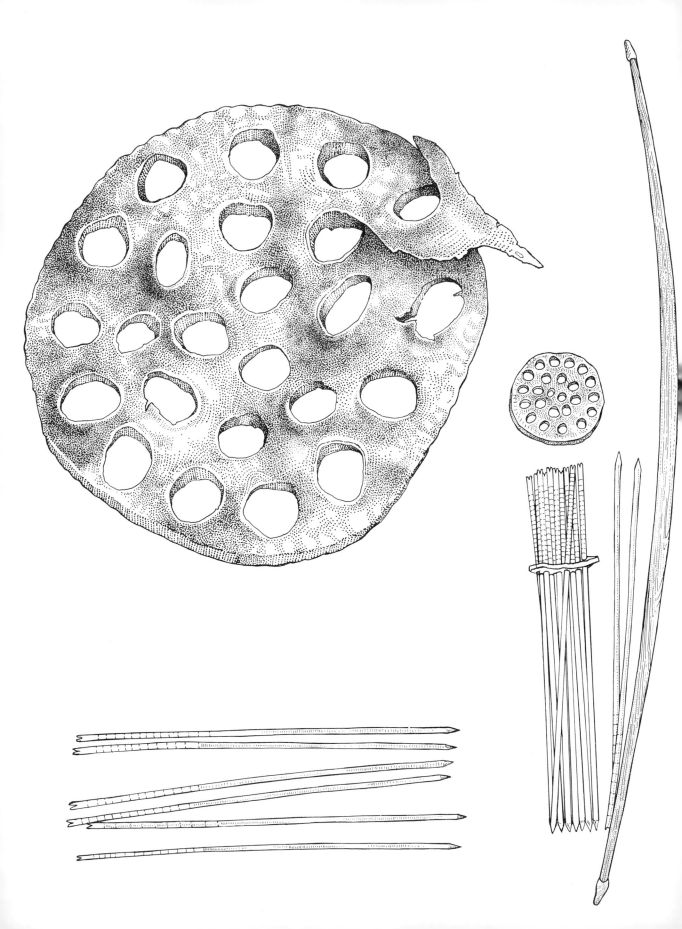

the midship section of the hull; to recover the artefacts in this area and continue the survey of the hull for ultimate recovery in 1982 . . . Many tons of silt were removed and around 3,000 objects recovered. This rich haul included many arrows, in fact one chest contained nearly 1,000 with only war heads and flight feathers missing. Also recovered: two pocket sundials, many rigging blocks (with most of them the sheaves still turn), beautiful sword scabbards, rope, longbows, guns, pikes etc.

The English military supremacy in archery was widely recognized throughout the continent and had proved its deadly efficiency at Crecy, Poitiers, Agincourt and many other battlefields. The six-foot long bow made of yew, with arrows of poplar, remained supreme until superseded by the hand gun; a devastating hail of arrows cleared the decks of an enemy warship. Prior to the discovery of so many aboard the *Mary Rose*, very few out of the myriads of bows that were made had survived, and two of those were recovered from another wreck which had sunk in the Thames – also in the reign of Henry VIII.

It has sometimes been said, erroneously, because of the success of his Norman archers at the Battle of Hastings, that William the Conqueror introduced the bow to England – but this was far from the case. The long bow had reached these shores centuries before, probably from Scandinavia, and archery had been widely practised since the Middle Ages. All men between 16 and 60 were compelled to practise it, and it reached its highest point of development during the Hundred Years War. The archers aboard the *Mary Rose* (many of whom have been found lying at their quarters with bows, quiver and arrows alongside them) were among the flower of Henry's troops and a bane to the French.

With the full cast of the bow it was deadly up to 300 yards, would pierce armour, and penetrate the thick sides of oak ships up to several inches. The great secret of this power and efficiency was that the English archer did not, like the French, "draw" the bow, but "bent it" – hence the expression "bending the bow". Rather than keeping his left hand steady and drawing with his right, the English archer kept his right hand at rest and laid the whole weight of his body into the horns of the bow. Hugh Latimer, the great churchman, described how his father in the reign of Henry VII taught him "not to draw with strength of arms as divers other nations do but with the strength of the body". It was a difficult art and not all could master it. His father taught him from an early age "how to draw, how to lay my body into the bow . . . I had my bows brought to me according to my age and strength; as I increased in them, so my bows were made bigger and bigger. For men shall never shoot well unless they be brought up to it."

A bow is usually assessed by its "weight", by which is meant the number of pounds required when applied to the string to draw back to the head an arrow of 28 inches or so. Curved tips of horn were used for the nocks at each end: neither these horned tips nor the bowstrings have survived their prolonged immersion (although it is possible that some may be recovered among boxes in the hold). R. P. Elmer writing of archery in 1932 gives a weight of about 55 to 60 pounds as being excellent "when in strong hands" at 100 yards. The cast of the old, English, long yew bow, of some 300 yards, required a weight of 100 pounds or more.

When training at long range, the archers fired at a white cloth stretched over a hoop which was known as a clout. Shakespeare has the words: "A' would have clapped i' the clout at twelve score, and carried you a forehand shaft a fourteen and fourteen and a half." The forehand shaft is one fired no higher than can be sighted over by the eye, and the distance is about 290 yards. An underhand shaft at an elevation of some $45°$ would have carried a great deal further – and still have been lethal.

The standard English bow of about six feet was a carefully designed product of that specialist, the bowyer: half round on the belly or face, it is almost flat on the back, and the whole taper is very gradual. One previous mystery (among so many others) that the Mary Rose has solved is a kind of leather disc pierced with 24 holes which, though a number of them had been found elsewhere, had hitherto defied identification. But, like the leather quivers they have been revealed still in situ: they were spacers, a means of spacing out the arrows so that their delicate feather flights were not damaged by jostling together. (Any modern English darts player can understand the importance of the flight . . .) Reaching back over his shoulder with his right hand, the archer could take another arrow, in good condition, from his quiver. It has been calculated that a skilled archer could get off some six rounds a minute, and it is probable that, before going into action, "clips" of these arrows in their spacers were ready around the firing positions so that – once a quiver was exhausted – a new "clip" could be picked up and inserted in the quiver, and the archer had fresh ammunition at the ready.

No one, however tough their fingertips and skin, can take for long the twanging pressure of the hempen string on the right-hand fingers, or the left forearm as the string grazes past. A leather glove was used for the right hand, or separate tips of leather for the fingers, while the wrist of the left, bow-arm was protected by a cuff of leather laced to the arm. Some of these also have been found aboard the Mary Rose, two of them elaborately decorated. Senior archers – like musket- and rifle-men in later centuries – were men of importance. They could determine a battle.

133

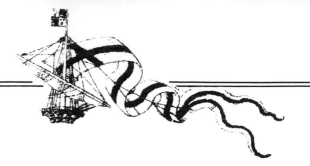

14. The Trust of the 'Mary Rose'

As THE TEAM got down deeper into the hull of the *Mary Rose* the whisper of the past became a voice, then a great murmur of many voices. The divers and the archaeologists were hearing a sound straight out of the sixteenth century. But, behind the day and the month and the year of 1545, the resurrection of the *Mary Rose* required a driving force of intelligence. This was provided by the *Mary Rose* Trust.

Richard Harrison, who had joined the *Mary Rose* Committee in 1975, became the first executive director of the Trust, co-ordinating all the activities, which were now expanding almost as fast as the relics from the ship were coming to the surface. While the work of divers may seem romantic and the work of archaeologists intellectually exciting, the steady background work of the organisation was, and still is, the essential backbone of the *Mary Rose* project. As Sir Eric Drake wrote in his Chairman's message in the report for 1980:

> The results of the excavation programme to date are exciting indeed and have enormously increased our knowledge both of the ship and life aboard her. Research has continued during the year upon the method of recovering the hull and its subsequent preservation, while progress continues to be made in the conservation of the numerous artefacts

Adrian Barak, one of the Trust's most experienced diver/archaeologists, joined the project in 1973.

already recovered . . . The Trust is especially indebted to all its supporters both in Britain and overseas, in particular to the British Sub Aqua Club, and to all those staff and voluntary workers whose dedication has made possible the great progress already achieved . . .

The reference to the voluntary workers and supporters, not only from Britain but other countries, emphasizes the fact that the *Mary Rose* had now achieved international significance. Richard Harrison in the executive director's report made the point that: "The first weeks of 1980 saw the first major review of progress towards meeting the objectives of the Trust, established 12 months earlier to excavate and recover the hull of the *Mary Rose* and to establish a *Mary Rose* Museum in Portsmouth." The first step towards the latter had been the opening at Southsea Castle of a preview, as it were, of the artefacts that were being raised from the ship: a foretaste of what was to follow, and what has continued to follow in rapid succession in subsequent years. This was to be enhanced by television: scenes received aboard the *Sleipner* were transmitted directly to Southsea Castle, so that visitors could see what was happening below the sea, as the divers worked. The uncovering of Tutankhamen's tomb was swathed in mystery, but the opening up of the *Mary Rose* was witnessed as it was in fact taking place.

In the summer of 1980 the *Mary Rose* Development Trust came into being. Ian Dahl, a senior executive at Marks and Spencers, now joined the team to give his business expertise to the sole task of securing that all-important lifeline to the whole project – money. The maintenance of the *Sleipner*, with all its attendant gear and machinery for the support of the divers and for raising objects from the seabed, cost many thousands a year; so did all the equipment needed in Warblington Street and elsewhere, Underwater archaeology is not conducted without a great deal of expense.

Richard Harrison wrote in his Report for 1980:

> The much-needed conservation facility was established, consisting of a research and development team (comprising a scientist, conservator and a technician) funded from a Leverhulme Trust grant, and a conservation team (comprising a conservator and two technicians) appointed as part of the Portsmouth City Museums Conservation Department. By the end of the year, this crucial element in the Trust's resources was fully operational and making a significant contribution to the preservation of the material recovered from the site.

1980 also saw the first full year of the operation of the Trust's Trading Company – selling copies of artefacts from those found aboard the *Mary Rose*, as well as pictures and other mementoes connected with the ship.

The excavation of the barber-surgeon's cabin was one of the greatest revelations of 1980: jars for ointments, handles for amputation saws, a bleeding bowl, medicine bottles, turned wooden containers, razors, a heavy wooden mortar for mixing drugs, and many other things associated with medicine at sea. Even the velvet coif worn by the barber surgeon, as evidence of his belonging to the guild, was preserved and has been restored. Clearly, as the finds from the *Mary Rose* have revealed, the medical art in the time of King Henry VIII was a great deal more advanced than had hitherto been supposed. A wooden mallet came to light along with so much else, and it has been conjectured that this may have been used in connection with amputation instruments. It is quite possible though that it had another purpose. At this time in the sixteenth century the most advanced

A drawing of the Barber Surgeon's velvet coif found aboard the Mary Rose. *The illustration on pages 62–63 shows members of the Barber Surgeons, wearing their coifs, being presented with a charter by Henry VIII. The Barber Surgeon was the ship's doctor Overleaf: Objects found in the Barber Surgeon's cabin include a bleeding bowl, a saw, a urethral syringe and a wooden mallet – perhaps used to anaesthetize the patient!*

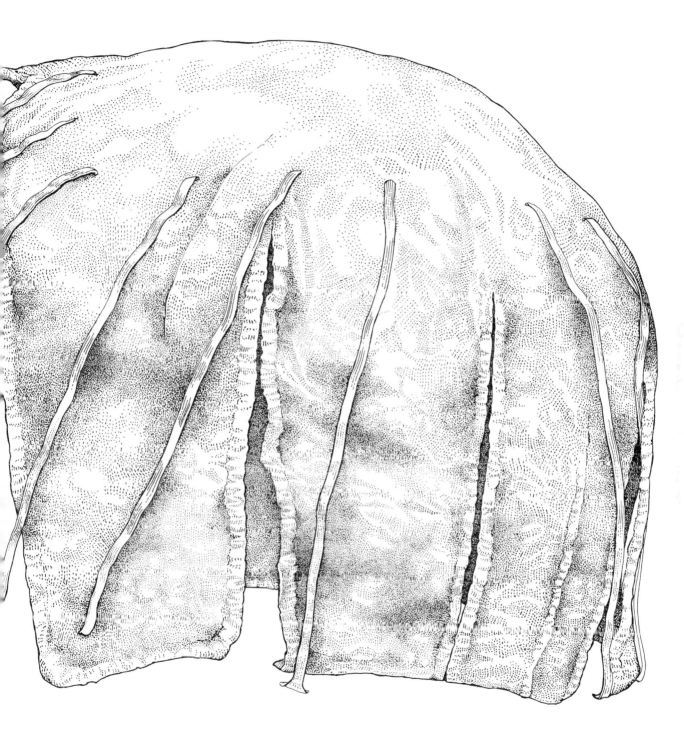

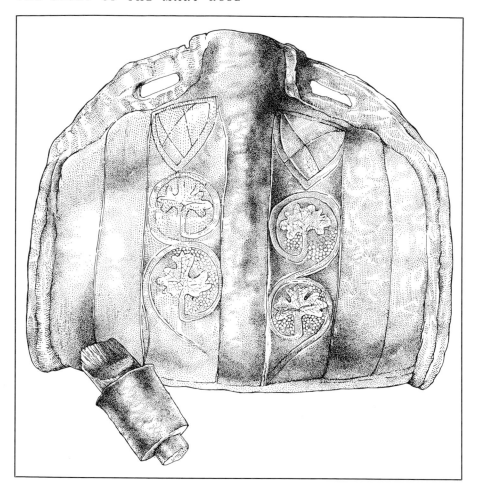

practitioners of medicine in the western world were the Knights of Malta, the Hospitallers of St. John, to whom many physicians looked for instruction. Alcohol and the narcotic sponge were used for inducing loss of consciousness, the latter being soaked in opium-poppy solution and other drugs. The patient took this sponge in his mouth and sucked it until the combination of the fumes rendered him unconscious. There was, however, another very simple but efficacious method of "putting a patient out" – probably the world's original anaesthetic. Dr. Paul Cassar writes in his *Medical History of Malta*: "The hammer-stroke was also practised. The patient's head was encased in a sort of helmet on which the surgeon delivered a good blow with a wooden hammer in such a way as to stun the patient into insensibility and thus enable him to go through the operation without suffering any pain." It is very doubtful if the medical art of Henry VIII's England was more

Far left: A drawing of a
leather flask.
Left: The Barber Surgeon's
urethral syringe.
Right: A powder horn
dispenser lid.

advanced than that of the renowned Knights Hospitaller.

One of the other artefacts recovered, almost certainly part of the barber-surgeon's equipment, is a delicate pair of brass scales, probably used for measuring out drugs or other medicinal effects. It is not surprising that among the finds were two urethral syringes: venereal diseases have always been rife among soldiers and sailors and "the pox" was prevalent in the six-teenth century. Syphilis, which was to be the scourge of Europe for many centuries (and which European sailors would spread all over the world) was first recorded by a Spanish physician in Barcelona in 1493. It is still debated by medical historians, but its origin seems to date from the Columbian discovery of America. There is no reference to it in classical literature, but by the sixteenth century Europe was invaded by syphilis. It may be that, when the anatomical investigation of the many skeletons found aboard the *Mary Rose*

142

A drawing of a leather-bound book found on board.

is complete, it will be found that some of the teeth show evidence of the disease. But this is mere conjecture.

Throughout 1980 the cannon, the leather shoes, leather corselets, buckets, rigging gear, glass and pewterware, continued to come to the surface. More was being learned about the *Mary Rose* than perhaps even those who sailed aboard her ever knew. The visitors of the twentieth century were taking a dispassionate look at a sixteenth-century "time-capsule". But some visitors were sometimes a little naive. Astonishment was voiced at the intricacy and delicacy of some of the objects – as if the moderns had forgotten that this was the world of the High Renaissance. Leonardo da Vinci had died 26 years before the *Mary Rose* sank: as an old man he had been at the court of Henry VIII's enemy, King Francis of France. The splendours and intricacies of Renaissance jewellery (some of which can be seen in portraits of Henry VIII himself) should have alerted commentators to the fact that in many respects the Tudor age was considerably more able and sophisticated than our own. Archaeologists who have worked among great ancient civilisations know that the fact that turners could make good wooden bowls and woodworkers other excellent wooden objects (treen) should amaze nobody. The amazing thing is that they were recovered from a previously submerged wreck that Alexander McKee had discovered some years before.

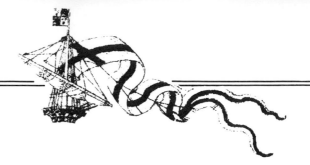

15. The Underwater World

AS THE DIVERS and archaeologists got deeper into the wreck, and more and more articles were retrieved, the ancient hull of the *Mary Rose* became a haven for sea life.

Here is an expert voice on the marine world that now began to inhabit the wreck of King Henry VIII's battleship:

Fish abound on the site . . . Pollack and pout, well known inhabitants of underwater structures, are always to be found. Shoals of large pollack congregate around the tops of the airlift searching for food in the clouds of debris. The smaller bib pout, in their thousands, form solid walls of fish around the piled timbers and in the shelter of the support vessel, *Sleipner*. More surprising is the group of about 30 magnificent bass, the largest of which is nearly a metre in length! These beautiful fish, usually no more than a fleeting glimpse in the surf, cruise around within a few feet of working divers. Bottom living fish such as dragonets and gobies merge well with the grey Tudor clay of the spoil heaps, taking advantage of small worms and other animals disturbed by the excavation. Blennies and bullheads prefer the seclusion of crevices between the timbers, when they can find one that is not occupied by a crab or lobster!

Edible crabs, swimming crabs and squat lobsters live in closer proximity than their aggressive behaviour might normally permit. As they can retreat deeply into cracks between planks, they do not seem to worry how close their next door neighbour is. It is doubtful that any harm is done to the wreck by this as the crabs and lobsters are nearly all small.

The timbers, once uncovered, are quickly eroded by bacteria, marine fungi and "gribble", a small isopod crustacean. This leaves a rough surface, ideal for the settlement of anemones, hydroids, sea squirts and bryozoans which, at certain times of year, produce considerable cover. This does not appear to cause any further deterioration, in fact it may even protect it from more voracious wood borers such as the dreaded Teredo.

The marine life of the Solent has wasted no time in taking advantage of this oasis in a desert of mud. It is now the turn of the biologist to benefit from further excavation bringing continued colonisation. (Jenny Mallinson, The Department of Oceanography, The University of Southampton.)

This interesting assessment of the marine life that now began to invade the *Mary Rose*, as she was freed of the protective sediment which had preserved her for so many centuries, has only one fault: it errs on the side of optimism. These words are being written in the last days of 1981 and already it is clearly seen that it is essential, if the hull is to be raised, that it is done in 1982. Now that the wreck is so exposed, the action of currents in the Solent together with the marine life can only cause considerable deterioration: indeed it is probable that yet another winter after that of 1981/2 would lead to the hull being virtually unsalvageable. Should teredo be present in the area (doubtful, but as indicated earlier, quite possible) it would be a disaster. Nothing except metal sheathing, such as copper on a hull, will keep out this voracious worm which enters a wooden hull or other wooden object almost invisibly and then eats its way along planking in a long scaly tube.

In 1980 alone some 3,000 objects were recovered, among them two pocket sundials. These had once held a very small compass so that the owner could accurately orientate them when taking a reading. They were the forerunners of the later pocket watch and the modern wristwatch, though one suspects that there must have been many days in an English channel summer when they would have been of little or no use.

Among the objects which had been found in the early days of the 1970s was a protractor, suggesting that navigation was taken seriously and that charts were in use; although none have yet come to light, they may yet do so from some box yet to be recovered. Then in 1980 and 1981 further discoveries were made which will interest all navigators: first one compass was found and then a further two, one of which was extremely well preserved and mounted in gimbals. The compass had been known for many

Left: A pocket sun-dial from the Mary Rose *which served instead of a wrist-watch in the Tudor era.*
Right: A pair of dividers and a slate protractor both of which were used in navigation.

centuries, but the earliest English example found up till now was some two hundred years later in date than this example from the *Mary Rose*.

The town of Amalfi in Italy was traditionally credited with the invention of the mariners' magnetic compass and there is an early twelfth-century reference by an Italian poet which seems to confirm this. Nevertheless the compasses from Henry VIII's warship are the oldest known of in northern Europe. The master or captain would undoubtedly have had one to consult, the steersman a second, and this third, which is in the best state of preservation, was probably a spare since it was discovered in a sea chest in the bow castle.

Dividers have also been found which, taken in conjunction with the protractor and the sophisticated compass, seem almost to confirm the use of charts. Indeed, there is no reason why an important warship of this type

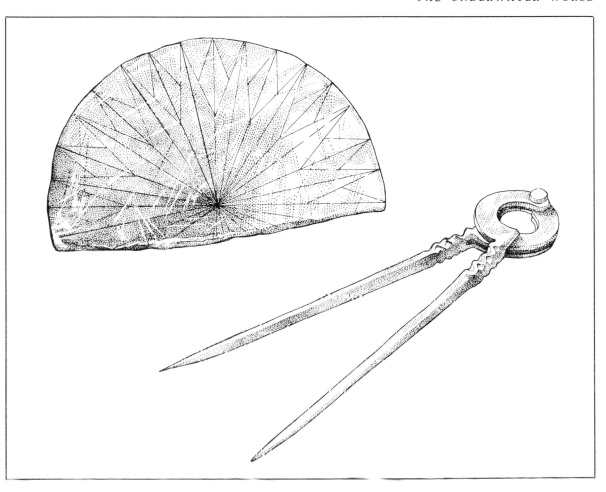

would not have been adequately equipped with charts. The first reference to a chart on shipboard occurs in 1270 – again in the Mediterranean – when St. Louis, the French king, consulted one when he was on his way to North Africa with a crusading army. The oldest surviving maritime chart, the *Carta Pisana*, is dated c. 1275.

Mrs Margaret Rule writes in a Progress Report in September 1981.

On the weather deck of the ship and on the main deck, a mixture of bronze and iron guns have been exposed, all complete with their carriages. Also now visible on the weather deck is a spare iron anchor.

As the divers work their way aft, a series of compartments – tiny box rooms between the gun stations – are being revealed on the main deck beneath the stern castle. Here, chests are being recovered containing selections of personal items. One chest even contained fishing tackle – lines, weights and floats. Clothing items include leather jerkins, shoes and boots; fabric items include a beret-style hat and a woollen stocking.

Among the small metallic items recovered and now conserved have been brass thimbles used by a sailmaker, an apothecary's balance – and the brass dispenser of a powder horn. This elaborate device contains a spring-operated mechanism designed to deliver a precise amount of powder through a nozzle mounted on the top of the artefact. Carved bone items are now being recovered – including a diminutive manicure set and an exquisitely-carved plaque bearing a representation of two angels in high relief; it was probably a book-spine decoration.

On the human side of simple Tudor life a number of very fine-toothed pocket combs – combs which would hardly be used just for tidying the hair – have come to light. Personal hygiene was difficult to maintain in those days, as indeed it was for centuries, and these combs were undoubtedly used for ridding the hair of fleas, nits and head lice. Generally speaking, people were bathed three times in their lives: on being born, on the marriage day, and on death. A visitor from the twentieth century would have felt uncomfortable in their presence, and one understands why the pomander, containing its ball of aromatic substances, came into fashion among the upper classes who could afford such things.

The rigging of large ships in these days was still extremely complex and a mass of material has come to light within the bo'sun's stores, while a great deal more lies under the starboard side of the hull where it fell when the first attempts at salvage broke the mainmast. The design of ships was still in a state of transition and the *Mary Rose* was caught up in the midst of these changes. It may be that, when everything has been studied, more will be learned about the way in which ships of this period were rigged. Later, when the British followed the Portuguese and Spaniards out into the Atlantic heading for the New World, everything would advisedly have been simplified to cope with the new conditions of the great ocean. The caravels of Portugal's Prince Henry the Navigator had shown the way, and soon the medieval atmosphere that still surrounded ships like the *Mary Rose* would yield to a new scientific precision. It may well be that the arguments among the many experts aboard the *Mary Rose* – "too many cooks" quarrelling about how best to handle things – contributed to her downfall.

One of the most interesting finds in this direction has been the large turned wooden parrel trucks, which resemble a giant necklace. Falconer's *Marine Dictionary* of 1780 (when things had greatly simplified over the centuries) opens a long description thus: "a machine used to fasten the sail-yards of a

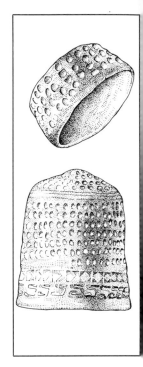

Artist's drawings of artefacts found aboard the Mary Rose: *above, a brass thimble; right above, a small pot and ear scoops; right, below, the manicure set.*

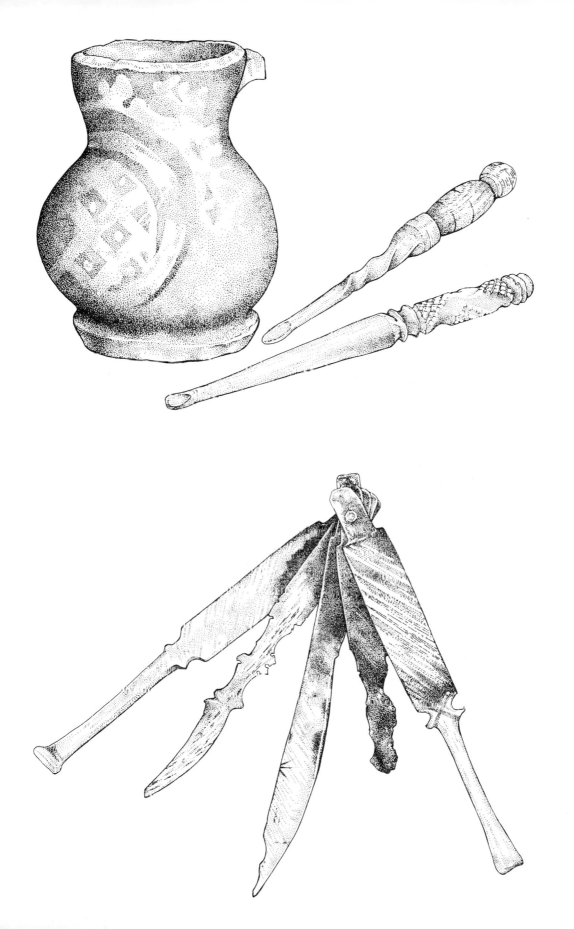

ship to the masts, in such a manner as that they may be easily hoisted thereon, as occasion requires.'' But it was not easy in Tudor times before the whole systems of rigging had been refined and one expert confirms that ''the method of fitting parrels is not definitely known . . .'' On gaff-rigged cutters, which are still sometimes to be found, they have no purpose but to enable the mainsail to slide easily up and down the mast when hoisting or lowering sail. But on squaresails of the type that the *Mary Rose* carried there had not only to be a hoist but a downhaul and various rope-leads to the deck. Few modern sailors (however experienced in canvas and rope) could have learned the system of the running rigging in this Tudor battleship in less than a number of weeks. It may be that the *Mary Rose*, when her rigging is carefully examined by expert mariners who understand sail, will reveal some more secrets. In the meantime one can admire the precision and craftsmanship of the men who built her and turned these mighty parrels.

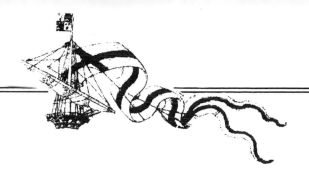

16. Archæology & Recovery

By the end of the summer of 1981 H.R.H. Prince Charles, President of the *Mary Rose* Trust, had made eight dives upon the ship. It is fascinating to think that his was the first royal hand or foot to touch the deck of the warship since Henry VIII himself in 1545. Thus was restored a royal presence to the old vessel and a message, as it were, transmitted that – whatever had happened in Europe and elsewhere – in Britain there was still a monarchy. The old king would have approved.

The *Tudor News* published in Portsmouth gives the following account of an interview with Prince Charles about diving on the *Mary Rose*:

He told an interviewer: "I do rather enjoy diving anyway – although the Solent is not actually the world's nicest place to dive. It's awfully murky . . . rather like swimming about in lentil soup because tidal movements stir up all this sediment . . . The first time I could see about ten or fifteen feet; last year, I suppose, about six to ten feet, but it takes time to accustom your eyesight to the light and then slowly things become more obvious.

"It is very much a business of groping your way round and following the marks that they've laid out and timbers, but terribly difficult to orientate oneself to which way the ship is lying and which way up it all is.

"Because it is lying on its starboard side at an angle of 60 degrees you have to try and visualize that angle when under water . . .

"But it was rivetting going around and seeing the timbers which were in a marvellous state of preservation. The transom, part of the stern, you could see quite easily.

"I was swimming along quite happily poking around when I looked down into a hole; suddenly I came face to face with a skull. I must say it did give me quite a fright . . . this skull marvellously preserved, beautiful teeth, absolutely perfect.

"Margaret Rule who was swimming with me wrote down on the board that it was the skull of a longbowman, she thought, because they had found next to this skull and bones some perfectly preserved longbows, unstrung, together with a quiver of arrows.

"I happen to be one of those people who are rivetted by history and I like to feel I have a sense of history. Obviously it's even more intriguing when it's there as a living example.

"So, for me it was a great thrill. A feeling of connection, as it were, with Henry VIII made it even more intriguing. I think historically the *Mary Rose* is important and will give people enormous pleasure and excitement to see what our ancestors put up with, how they lived at sea and everything else."

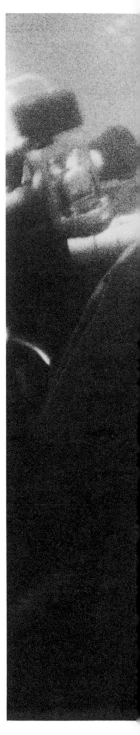

In the working year of 1980 the deck planking of the weather deck was removed: this for three reasons. The divers and diving archaeologists were now getting deeper into the hull and their safety was imperilled by the conditions of the deck fastenings above them. The removal of the planking made easier the removal of articles from the protecting silt that had so long covered them. Thirdly, it was regarded that the removal of these beams and planks would facilitate the ultimate recovery of the hull itself. The position of all these timbers was scientifically recorded and annotated so that in due course they could be put back again exactly as the Tudor craftsmen had laid them. They will be held in a stable condition and not conserved until after the whole hull is recovered, and it can be treated as an integral unit.

In some cases this chronicling of the wooden structures was complicated by the fact that the shipwrights of the *Mary Rose* had patched up pieces here and there as defects developed. It must be remembered that, although she had had an extensive refit, she was not a new ship on the day that she heeled over and sank. She was 14 years old in 1525, as a list of the king's ships states plainly, and she went down 20 years later. This is a great age for a wooden sailing vessel (although the writer has sailed in one that was over 40 years old). But the *Mary Rose* had had more than the conventional refit: she had been almost completely converted, from an old-style carrack fitted with

guns, to a broadside warship which foreshadowed all warships until the Age of Steam put paid to them in the nineteenth century.

The excavation of the *Mary Rose* has of course exposed her. The archaeological director, Mrs. Margaret Rule, wrote in a report on 2 February 1981:

> It was anticipated that the deepest excavation would be five metres deep and it was proposed to reinforce the deck beams as the excavation proceeded with Acrow-props supported on wooden blocks on each beam. *As the excavation progressed it was realized that the loss of iron fastenings which had formerly secured the deck planks to the beams and ledges made the whole structure inherently weak and when the silts were removed from the decks there was a tendency for the deck planks to become displaced and to slip downwards across the deck beams.* [My italics. E.B.]

Deterioration of her iron fastenings had occurred.

Sometimes in this period ships were entirely fastened by wooden treenails, but the advanced technology of Henry VIII's England – with its sophisticated iron and bronze cannon alone – had ensured that much of this work was achieved with the aid of iron bolts. Since iron deteriorates rapidly in salt water , it was now clear that the whole of the internal structure would have to be dismantled, and that the hull (before it could be raised) would have to receive modern longitudinal and athwartships bracing; otherwise it would break up when the time came for lifting the ship. The necessity for carefully removing large sections of the internal structure imposed a great strain on the divers in 1980–81 and to some extent delayed operations. The *Wasa* which had been brought ashore with much of her mud and silt inside her had, in some respects, proved easier: she was at least a whole ship, whereas the much older *Mary Rose* is little more than her starboard side – half a walnut shell in fact. "However," as Mrs. Rule put in this report, "there will be a bonus, it is a much more straightforward problem to support a shallow empty hull of the ship by athwartships spacing and longitudinal bracing than it would have been to support decks of unknown strength and unknown weight if they had been left in position."

The portrait of the Tudor Age that emerges from the *Mary Rose* is a world that was based around leather and wood (with iron and bronze becoming available for weapons of war). But, except for the diversity and complexity of the cannon, this should surprise no one. The Renaissance had come late to the island of Britain and many have unthinkingly assumed that this was still almost a medieval world. The cultural and scientific tides emanating from Italy and sweeping through France had, given improved marine communications (despite the setbacks of wars), already washed the island in the

north. In fact, as so often (and as we can see in our own sad age), the effects of war were to speed up metallurgy and many technical advances. In the long history of "the most dangerous animal in the world" wars, which have led to the collapse of dynasties and empires, have also led to an improvement in weaponry. Hence the great and beautiful guns aboard the *Mary Rose*; hence also the "spin-off" of metalworking techniques into the lives of ordinary private citizens. The full flood of the Renaissance would be felt in England in the Elizabethan Age – causing that flowering in architecture and literature, jewellery and ships – but its advancing waters can already be felt in the man-made objects that have come up in their thousands from the wreck of this for so long forgotten vessel.

To list artefacts (as archaeologists and museum curators like to call them) is somewhat tedious. A list of flowers in a garden – complete with their Latin

HRH the Prince of Wales visiting the Mary Rose Trust. From left to right: Lieutenant-Commander Peter Whitlock, Richard Harrison, Sir Eric Drake, Chairman, the Prince, and Debbie Fulford, the Trust's senior illustrator. In the background ex-king Constantine of Greece.

156

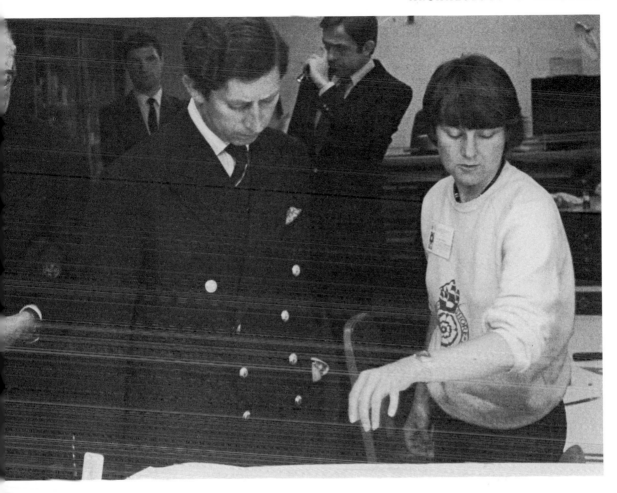

names – means little except to a professional gardener with a classical education. The *Mary Rose* when she put out to sea on that summer day, however, was a living portrait of the Tudor world as it was lived by officers, seamen and the soldiery. Aft, for the officers, were musical instruments, a pewter jug, gold coins and smooth well-turned wooden bowls; forward lie more roughly turned wooden tableware, nit combs, a simple gaming board and all the evidences of a rougher way of life. Once again, this should surprise nobody. "Back aft" and "Up forrard" have for centuries been terms which in the Navy designated the great differences between officers and men.

"A personal chest of bows and arrows has also been found," writes Mrs. Margaret Rule in 1981, "and it will be interesting to study the range of weapons used by one archer. Among other items stored in chests are cross

bow bolts, planes, sheathed knives, leather clothing and two fine gold coins . . . Clearly defined storage compartments on the orlop deck contain rope, barrels of pitch or tar, lanterns, rigging blocks, firewood, sailcloth.''

William Shakespeare, writing in *The Tempest*, some seventy years after the death of the *Mary Rose*, evokes the rough and simple world known to these seamen – and, indeed, known to sailors ever since:

> "The master, the swabber, the boatswain and I,
>   The gunner and his mate,
> Lov'd Mall, Meg, and Marian and Margery,
>   But none of us car'd for Kate;
>   For she had a tongue with a tang,
>   Would cry to a sailor, 'Go hang!'
> She loved not the savour of tar nor of pitch,
> Yet a tailor might scratch her where-e'er she did itch:
> Then to sea, boys, and let her go hang.''

Despite the passing of centuries, our dead ancestors were not so very different from ourselves.

But, between the barber-surgeon's urethral syringe, between the musical instruments and the gaming board, lie the real reason for these mens' presence aboard the *Mary Rose*. There lie the guns.

Left: One of the muzzle loading bronze guns being raised.
Right: A heavily encrusted iron gun being hoisted aboard the Sleipner, using an air bag which can be seen to the left of the picture.
Below: An historic moment, as a wooden gun carriage from the Mary Rose is swung aboard the recovery vessel.

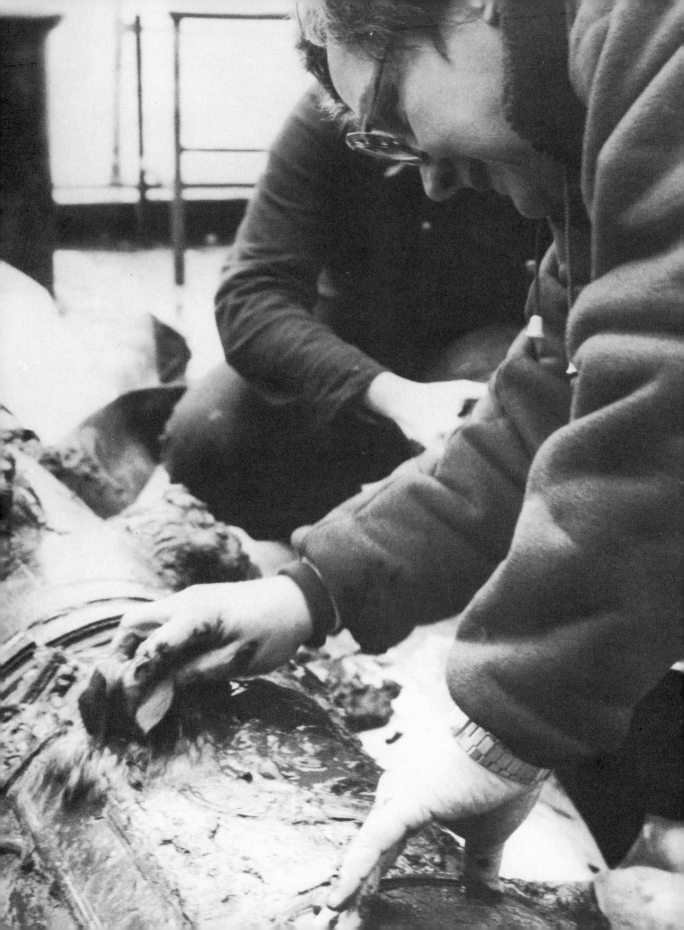

Left: Margaret Rule closely examines the heraldic device on one of the newly raised bronze muzzle loading guns.
Above Right: A close inspection of the inside of a muzzle loading gun.
Below Right: Visitors to Southsea Museum looking at some of the breech-loading iron guns recovered from the Mary Rose. In the background one of the heavier bronze muzzle-loaders and various sizes of shot.
Below: A bronze bastard.

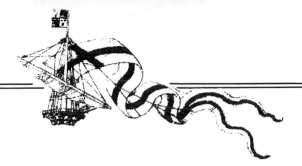

17. Preserving the Past

Richard Harrison standing in the gun store with some of the many guns raised from the Mary Rose.

CONSERVATION IS the essence of the *Mary Rose* project. All the efforts of the divers, the archaeologists, the office staff, the fund raising team, and the public relations section, would be nullified without the work of the conservation team. The objects that come up from the sea, whether wood, iron, bronze or leather, all need special treatment to ensure that they can survive in the environment which they left so many centuries ago – and which is now a hostile environment. Beneath the sea they have been impregnated with salts, attacked by marine borers and micro-organisms, but under the layers of mud and silt they have enjoyed a stable situation. To be lifted and exposed to the effects of the air means that an almost instant change begins to take place within the objects. Perhaps iron is the worst, but even glass – which many might think impervious to salt water – needs strict attention.

The first work is done aboard the *Sleipner* where Sam Dooley, who has been 29 years in deep-sea salvage work, presides as master. The object of the vessel is not only to form an efficient working platform but also to provide the archaeologists with their first glimpse of articles as they are recovered. Here also is done the first preliminary work not only of assessing the finds but also of starting them on the long road towards total conservation. Sam Dooley, who was formerly in the Navy, is an enthusiast for his job and delights in the occasions when a big gun comes to the surface. "That's

165

really something to see."

Towed out in the early spring before the diving season starts, the *Sleipner* has been fitted with heavy mooring winches so that she can stay on her fixed anchorage throughout the working season – gales notwithstanding. The south-westerlies do not trouble her for where she lies she is in the lee of the Isle of Wight, but a strong south-east gale can make life very uncomfortable for those aboard. Apart from Sam Dooley, the master, there are an engineer, a watch-keeper officer and a seaman permanently aboard.

Reliefs come and go by boat, as do the recovered objects and there are six boats a day between her and the shore. Others have to be ferried back and forth – on an average about 20 divers a day during the working season, although on occasions in the past there have been as many as 50. It is hard work, and the glamour of the retrieved articles from Henry VIII's old warship should not blind the visitor to the hazardous efforts that have led to their recovery. Apart from the visiting divers, all of whom have to be carefully instructed in procedures and record-keeping, there is Margaret Rule's permanent team who do two days on duty and one day off, weather permitting, throughout the season. In 1981 they carried on right into December: the Solent (as Prince Charles commented) is not the pleasantest place to dive and it can be imagined what temperatures and conditions the divers encountered.

During the working year of 1981 11,057 dives were logged and 9,216 man/hours were spent on the seabed. Apart from the 10 divers of the *Mary Rose*, working full-time, about half the dives were made by part-time volunteers coming from all over the world.

But when the diving is over and the objects retrieved – whether massive Tudor cannon or the humble leather shoes of seamen – then begins the work of conservation. An agreement between the Portsmouth City Museums and the *Mary Rose* Trust was made and a senior conservator and two technicians were appointed, their services being paid for by the Trust. Further to this, with the aid of a grant from the Leverhulme Trust, three people were also appointed, whose task was to examine conservation methods to treat the needs of underwater conditions. Leather, textiles and wood all involve a new and dispassionate approach to the problems, being delicate substances; but iron and glass, too, require a great deal of specialized thinking. Computers have, of course, helped enormously in evaluating situations which in earlier days would have proved extremely difficult.

Articles of wood and leather are placed in special freeze dryers to remove the water. But they then need preliminary treatment. Wood, for instance, needs to have its fibres refilled, as it were, which is done with polyethylene glycol, a water-soluble wax. For most items, cloth and rope especially, the

Above right: Amongst the sophisticated equipment used for conservation by the Mary Rose Trust is this freeze-drying chamber. Here the Project Conservator, Howard Murray, is placing a gaming board from the wreck in the chamber while Chris O'Shea, Portsmouth City Museum's senior conservation officer, looks on.
Below right: Howard Murray loading the freeze-drying chamber.

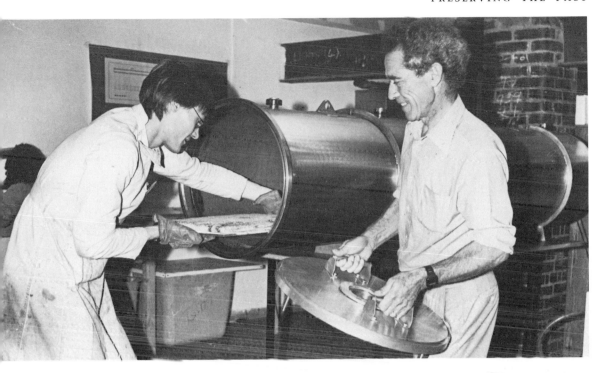

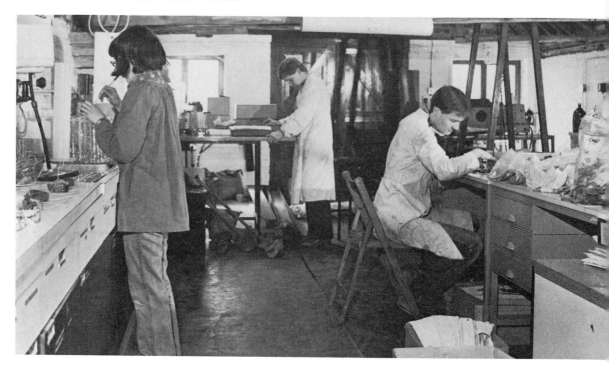

cascade system is used, whereby a constant stream of fresh water descends upon them – leaching out the salts and other impurities that have invaded them over the centuries. The same technique is also used on pottery and glass which, although on first being cleaned off appear to be in good condition, are also impregnated with salts, and if untreated will deteriorate at a rapid rate. Underwater archaeology is a far call from archaeology ashore. Those who have attended 'digs' in dry areas – the eastern Mediterranean lands for example – will have seen how even delicate objects emerge crisp and clear, even though they may have been buried 2000 years and more. With the *Mary Rose* it has been a battle, and on a new battlefield with almost every object.

Wrought iron objects from guns to minor items provide a great deal of trouble and concern, for the corrosion of the iron is worse than anything else. Although cast and wrought iron cannon are usually well preserved under

169

their layer of carbonates and silicates, small objects can almost vanish, leaving behind only a negative cast of what they were. But this too can be made use of, and a mould can be made from the "cast" (using plaster or silicone rubber). Small objects, when they are first cleaned up on the *Sleipner* and the air first hits, will even begin to "steam" within minutes of the atmosphere striking them.

But the large iron cannon provide the greatest problem – on account of their size as much as anything else. At first, when the encrustations and marine deposits are chipped away, the metal beneath appears as dark and shining as it was when the gunners of King Henry VIII last saw it. One is looking then with a Tudor eye at a Tudor gun as it was last seen in 1545. But rapidly a sinister change begins: the shiny dark surface begins to wither and turn brown. Before the witch's curse can take effect this sleeping beauty must be hurried to the shoreside unit where iron cannon are treated. In charge of this is Chris O'Shea, senior conservation officer of the Portsmouth Museums. The gun is pre-treated with caustic soda solution. It is also examined by gamma radiography to determine its structure, welds and so on. The next and major part of the operation is the use of the hydrogen furnace. The gun is loaded into the container and the process starts: flush with nitrogen, heat, then hydrogen, the temperature is raised to 400°F and there it remains for 40 to 100 hours. It is watched over like a child for 24 hours per day, and then it requires 24 hours for the furnace to cool. When the gun is unloaded from the furnace, the oxydized iron having been brought back to stable metallic iron, all is not yet over. Polyester resins are applied to toughen the structure and to prevent atmospheric corrosion. If it had a gun carriage, and that is restorable, then the modern visitor will be able to see this *Mary Rose* piece much as it was on that day in July 1545 when Sir George Carew headed out for action against the enemy.

The dedicated work that has gone into conservation work such as this (it is to be found among all the conservators at all levels) is a happy reminder that people will work long hours and in exhaustive detail for the sake of doing what they really care about. Ian Panter, for instance, is a fully qualified archaeological conservator, specializing in leather and glass. He explains how leather must receive the water treatment to leach out the impurities of centuries under the sea and that after this stage the leather, be it a bucket or a jerkin or a shoe, can be treated with polyethylene glycol. Unfortunately, while this consolidates the leather it does not restore flexibility, and further treatment is needed with the oils or fats that leather needs. Leather is now treated with bavon.

Iron salts from iron guns have percolated through the material and research has to be made how best to remove them. Further research is being

Left: A restored leather bucket.
Right: A variety of wooden objects, displayed after conservation.

made into the tanning process in Tudor times. (It is well known that in ancient days the tanning process was a very smelly one – excrement being used to soften the leather. At certain times and in certain countries stringent laws were laid down that a tannery might not be within a given distance of town, village or manor.) Ian Panter has dealt with leather jerkins where only the stitch-points in the leather show where once the chain mail was attached – the metal of course has long since disappeared. Sword scabbards of leather equally survive, though the swords have gone, but their hilts if of wood or non-ferrous metal have also survived. Apart from pouches, purses, shoes, leather arrow quivers, flasks and arrow spacers, one of the most interesting finds needing treatment was a pair of officer's thigh boots, all neatly folded up – clearly what later generations would have called "going ashore gear".

Dr. John Harvey, senior research scientist, whose speciality is wood, has much to say about these matters. It would seem that most of the *Mary Rose*'s rope was of hemp rather than flax. The texture of most of that which has been recovered seems to be too coarse for flax, although it would prove curious if none of the rope aboard the *Mary Rose* was flaxen for England had plenty of it available. Of the woods aboard the ship oak, as we have seen and as was to be expected, provided most of the structural parts of the ship. The second major wood was elm – "immemorial elms", as Tennyson called them, and one of the noblest of ship-woods. In half beams where replacements had been made the woods are assorted, for "Chippy" the carpenter had to make use of whatever was to hand when an immediate repair was called for.

As with almost everything else that has come up from the sea, reducing the salt content has been the first requirement. Iron and salt that had invaded the wood had to be swilled away first of all. Then, once cleared, the water loss had to be replaced by getting a wax content into the wood. This may be not over-difficult in small objects like treen, but in the case of the *Mary Rose* great timber knees and deck beams had to be removed. (There has most fortunately been only one fatality up to this date among the divers on the seabed, and this had nothing to do with working conditions or the very high standards of safety precautions.)

Left: One of the enormous rigging blocks found aboard the Mary Rose.
Above: Various sizes of stone, iron and lead shot found aboard the Mary Rose, *together with stone moulds for making lead shot.*

Small objects, though each one poses its own problem, were relatively easy to handle – favourite woods being beech and alder, while turned canisters were made of poplar. The arrows, as we know, were all made of poplar, but the crossbow quarrels were made of ash. Elm, as for centuries yet to come, was for the keel, while most large knees were also of elm as well as the wales, or strengthening pieces, to the gun carriages. It would be more than pleasant to welcome back as *revenants* some of these Tudor shipwrights, carpenters and treen-makers into our modern world of plastics. Their skill would be such that presumptuous modern man would realize that not all advances are technological.

Among the many interesting facts that have emerged from the *Mary Rose* is that every single gun, of whatever shape or size, has been found to be fully loaded. Not surprising, one might say, as she was just going into action. Since reloading was not exactly quick, the main thing was to hit the enemy with a hail of shot and ball at the earliest notice. Chris O'Shea, however, points out that he has investigated the guns of ships of much later date and found the same thing – even ships that had sunk in times of so-called 'peace'. It would seem that in the Narrow Seas when a man sailed out he had his pistol primed. The first salvo must always be ready at any time. The 'first strike' was all-important.

173

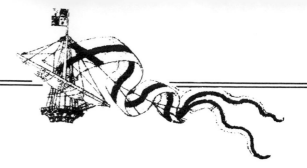

18. Finding, Recording & Identifying

THE *Mary Rose* was a warship, just leaving her home port.

One would not expect to find aboard her anything like those treasures which Robert Sténuit and his helpers found on the Armada galleass *Girona*, which was embarked upon the Enterprise of England, the intended conquest of the island, which would entail prolonged residence if successful and the payment of many troops. The *Mary Rose* was a bare ship stripped for action, and with no likelihood that, if the action was successful, she would have to proceed any further than the shores of France in pursuit of the enemy.

Hence results the absence of any distracting 'treasures' which might have given the press a field day, but which would have revealed far less about the life of the Tudor seaman than the wide cross-section that has been brought to the surface. One thing that is most noticeable about almost all the finds recovered to date is, in the aesthetic phrase, their 'fitness for use'. This is a simple and practical world of wool, wood and leather, everything there having been fashioned by experience over centuries so that there is no needless embellishment, but everything *works*. The most elaborate decoration is to be found on the large brass cannon, where the cost of the metal and the skills of the gunfounder have caused some elaboration to flower – although even here it is restrained. The full Renaissance-tide has not quite reached England's shores. Delicate work like the barber-surgeon's scales

Pat Edge, Volunteer Assistant, at work restoring some woollen fragments.

show not so much refinement as scientific precision. This is something which is demonstrated yet again in the spring-operated top of a powder horn, designed to measure out the correct amount of powder, but in no way to be 'fancy'.

In fact, in everything one sees one senses that peculiarly English feeling for form and material without elaboration. So, in subsequent centuries, when

175

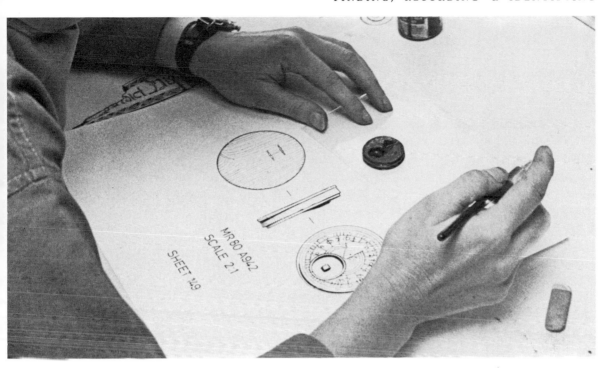

Left: Every significant artefact that has been recovered from the Mary Rose has been carefully drawn by Debbie Fulford and her team. Above: A close-up of Debbie Fulford's drawing of a pocket sun dial.

the French were making highly finished furniture of ormolu and inlay, the English cabinet-maker would be constructing his pieces – desks, bureaux or tables – with either local woods or imported mahogany, all with a sense of fitness for use. The few pewter spoons that have been preserved are simple and practical but they foreshadow a type and style that would go on being made for centuries. The works of this strange amalgam of northern peoples – largely Anglo-Saxons and Normans – are a far call from the greater elaboration to be found in more southern lands. They are also removed from the extreme elaboration of those Celts who had earlier dominated the culture of the island.

Andy Elkerton, finds supervisor aboard the *Sleipner*, is one of the first to deal with newly recovered objects. Initial cleaning and identification come first in his work, which he started in 1979. After the direct survey method under the water has identified the position of each object (exactly where it lay) it can be brought to the surface. Different types of sediment can give a general guide to area and depth. Whatever its condition or its function, every object is immediately sent ashore where expert analysis and computerized technology can at once be brought to bear upon it.

During his first year on the project he saw some 1000 objects of all kinds brought to the surface; during the second year more than 2000; and during

177

1981 more than 3000. These figures encompass man-made things alone and do not include the large amount of wooden structures that had to be dismantled. Each item, large or small, is recorded meticulously – the handles of weapons, the yew bows, the arrows, the cannon, and even the bones of long-dead men. The timbers come up carefully numbered, so that ultimately the jigshaw puzzle can be put together. "It is," says Elkerton, "often difficult with volunteer divers who come to the surface extremely excited over a find – and having to get from them the exact identity of an area!"

This is how it is all done at the fountainhead: the books and the papers for learned societies will follow later. You could not put Drake's voyage around the world into the same fine-meshed sieve, but in the twentieth century – under the new pressurized techniques – this is what has to be done. Elkerton works two days on, one day off, aboard the *Sleipner*: he prefers it this way for as he says: "Staying aboard is a good way of discussing at the end of the day all the problems that have come up. After the divers and others have left, there is a peaceful time to discuss what has happened – and what is likely to happen." The variety, he emphazises, is endless: it may be another cannon or an as yet indecipherable piece of a Tudor book. Some of those simple bone and wood carvings, with which sailors whiled away their time during the long hours of boredom when nothing was happening, have come up. Objects vary so much – from the fine-tongued Tudor combs of bone or of wood, to an encrusted cross of silver, which would totally disappear if its protective salts were removed.

"The skull impresses – induces thought." But any who may have imagined that the bones of the Captain or the Vice-Admiral would differentiate themselves from those of archers or seamen are living in a world of modern sentimentality. Bones are bones and, like Yorick's skull, will reveal no more than that. In the vast fraternity of the grave Carew's calcium deposits are identical with those of a humbler archer. The major part of the ship's company seem to have been middle-aged men – that is to say, by the standards of those days. Most, to judge by their teeth, were in their thirties: short and stocky men, with good teeth in the main, for imports of sugar had not yet affected their diet. Some, though, show evidence of rickets – calcium deficiency – and some of impacted molars. For centuries the Englishman would dull pain with alcohol of one sort or another, until the advent of opiates (laudanum best known of all) would enable them to dull themselves into insensibility. De Quincey and Coleridge, to instance but two writers centuries later, did not indulge in narcotics because, like modern youth, they wanted a 'high'; they took these soporofics because they were in pain. Life in general was "nasty, brutish, and short", and one must not imagine in some genial glow of false romance that the life of a bowman or seaman – or even

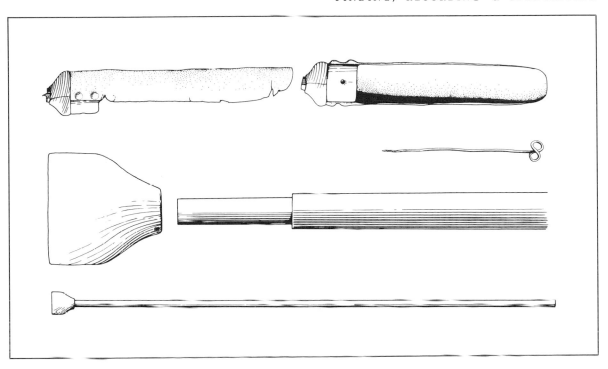

A wooden rammer, a gunpowder scoop and a bronze reamer – all items used by the gunners aboard the Mary Rose – are examples of Debbie Fulford's meticulous drawing.

Admiral – was anything comparable with what is known by the majority of the population four hundred years later. There stands between us the deep divide of Time and, though we may measure their bones and peruse the empty eyeholes of their skulls, we must not imagine that we have much knowledge of what they really thought.

Of course they considered their women, their children, the places where they lived: but we can suppose as much about Stone Age man as that. Although our ancestors, they are almost as remote from us as Inca Indians – and thus we must regard them: lying alone in the wreck of the *Mary Rose* on the seabed until modern man came down and moved them. Once the detailed investigations are over it is to be hoped that their bones will be returned to the deep sleep from which we have disturbed them. This, too, is a sentimentality – but a fitting one.

Every diver keeps a log of his or her activities, something which initially entailed a lot of paperwork and filing, but once again computerization is simplifying things. Meticulous accuracy while working on the ship means that even objects which were broken on the *Mary Rose*'s impact with the seabed and then separated can be checked and in due course related to one another even if found at different times and places. It is a giant jig-saw puzzle monitored by the most sophisticated modern techniques. The

179

diversity of the objects is the diversity of a world. To itemize would be tedious, but some indication must be given of how the things found range from the natural to the man-made. Only thus can one understand how a whole image of Tudor England went down with the *Mary Rose*, something which the enthusiasm of divers, the intellectual ingenuity of archaeologists and patient skill of conservators has resurrected.

Many men shaved, so there were razors, the cutting edge of course long since gone, but the handle and the flip-up part for the thumb showing that they were not dissimilar to those our grandfathers used. A pear-shaped sundial to be hung round the neck like an ornament had holes beneath it and a small compartment which may have served as a pomander. One cannot imagine that the smells aboard ship can have been tolerable to sensitive nostrils. Scatterings of leaves may indicate that some effort was made to counteract odours.

Apart from a mass of fish bones, there are chicken bones and (not surprisingly) rats' bones. The proverbial rats who "leave a sinking ship" do so not because of any special prescience, but because rats dwell in the bilges: they are the first to know when the water level is rising. In the case of the *Mary Rose* they had no forewarning. There was also a small dog on board but, curiously enough, so far no cats' bones have been found. "A cat may look at a king," said Alice – and one likes to think that perhaps there was aboard the *Mary Rose* a cat that once saw Henry VIII in all his finery.

The fine pewter flagon probably indicates the officers' table, where men had a taste for wine, but a wooden stave-built tyg, or drinking vessel, with a fliptop such as is ordinarily associated with German beer mugs portrays an ancient Anglo-Saxon style that leads one back to the days of the Vikings. There is no evidence that the Tudor seaman was undernourished; indeed he would seem to have been a great deal better fed than the sailors of Nelson's navy. Plum stones show that there was even fruit available. These men who battled only across the Narrow Seas were never far from a home port – not for them the long scurvy-ridden voyages across the Atlantic and into the Pacific. That would all come only too soon, and whole generations would have to learn about deep-sea victualling, water supplies, and the menace brought about by the absence of fresh vegetables and fruit.

The coordination apex of the pyramidal structure of the *Mary Rose* Trust on site is held by the archaeologist, Mrs. Margaret Rule, and several others. They stand at the point where, with the aid of skilled professional knowledge, they must attempt to put together all the information that comes pouring in. They must attempt to identify the finds, trace them to their original location, ascertain their usage aboard, ascribe them to their position in our knowledge of social life and ships of this period.

A diver with a video camera.

Except for the fine cannon and the most unusual breech-loaders, the objects that have come up from the *Mary Rose* are essentially mundane. This, as has been said, is not surprising: she was a warship going out to give battle just off her home port. The *Mary Rose* has to be viewed *in toto*: as she lies there, half a hull, with the things that were aboard her – just as they went down on that July day. Viewed item by item they may mean little to the untrained eye, but put all together and they produce a composite picture of a day in the life of a new type of warship in midsummer 1545. The conclusion must be all the stronger, therefore, that they must all be gathered together in one museum, a museum where they can be seen in relation to her hull.

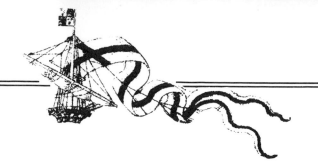

19. Past & Future

THE IDEA OF preserving a ship is not new in itself: it goes back as far as the days of Henry VIII's daughter, Elizabeth. In 1581, after the Queen had knighted Francis Drake on the deck of his famous warship the *Golden Hind*, following upon his voyage round the world, there was a great popular outcry for the vessel to be preserved. The Queen herself agreed that the *Golden Hind* should be kept as a national monument. Drake's ship was put into a dry berth at Deptford and lay there for many years but, alas, little was known about preserving wooden timbers ashore in those days, and she finally rotted to pieces. Ben Jonson in one of his comedies had a character remark: "We'll have our provided supper brought aboard Sir Francis Drake's ship that hath encompassed the world, where, with full cups and banquets, we will do sacrifice for a prosperous voyage . . ."

Mens' hearts and imaginations attach themselves to objects associated in some important way with their country's history: witness the aircraft, ships, tanks and other souvenirs of war that have been carefully restored in our own warlike century, and kept as memorials for the nation. Portsmouth, where it is hoped that a museum will house not only the thousands of objects from the *Mary Rose* but also her hull, is already graced with what is probably the most famous ship in the world: H.M.S. *Victory*. Dominant in her drydock, beautifully maintained, she represents the great age of Fighting

Sail. Some half a million visitors a year come to see the *Victory*, gaze in awe at those massive timbers, rigging and masts, and are roused from twentieth-century preoccupations to an understanding that they are standing on a ship where the history of the world was changed.

Portsmouth, as is only fitting, is in itself a maritime museum; although little of old Portsmouth itself remains after the devastating raids of World War Two. The city has its own flotilla of old ships. There is T.S. *Foudroyant*, which now serves as a youth training centre: she was built at Bombay in 1807. Soon there will be H.M.S. *Warrior*, another transitional ship, being Britain's first warship constructed entirely of iron. Built on the Thames in 1860, she is 400-foot long and has an immense weight of armour on her iron hull. Restoration work is being carried out on her in Hartlepool with a view to her joining the historic flotilla in Portsmouth. Like so many ships of her time, when steam was still not entirely trustworthy as a means of propulsion, she was also rigged with sail. Engines were mistrusted by a very conservative Admiralty long after they had been accepted in other marine spheres, and in 1878 H.M.S. *Gannet*, a steam and sail sloop, was built at Sheerness, familiar for years to yachtsmen on the Hamble river as T.S. *Mercury* (now closed). She too will form part of the floating museum at Portsmouth. Last but not least of these transitional vessels is the submarine H.M.S. *Alliance*, the last British submarine to be built for service in World War Two. In 1982 she is expected to be opened to the public at Gosport. Visitors unfamiliar with the conditions (lack of space, above all) in the old type of submarines will learn more about how their submariner fathers fought in the war than from many books. The conditions aboard H.M.S *Victory*, as is easy to see, were cramped in the extreme, but the nearest approximation to those aboard H.M.S. *Alliance* were probably the quarters aboard the *Mary Rose* – and the *Mary Rose* was not expected to be at sea for days on end. Those who say that the twentieth-century sailor could not endure the discomfort and overcrowding of the Tudor warship should pay a visit to this World War Two submarine – always bearing in mind that she had more space and comfort than many of her predecessors.

To see the *Mary Rose* in perspective is to see her in the company of her descendants. She is, to date, the earliest on the family tree and she brings with her innumerable examples of how life was lived in her days. There are still families in England who can trace their ancestry back to Tudor times – and even earlier – and some of the houses in which their ancestors lived are still standing, but none has the distinction of possessing thousands of artefacts and articles in daily use by them as does the *Mary Rose*.

It was fitting, then, that early in 1982 Henry VIII's warship was declared an historic monument by the Department of the Environment. Under the

terms of the Ancient Monuments and Archaeological Areas Act (1979) a number of important places and buildings have been preserved – but all of them on dry land. The *Mary Rose* is the first underwater site to be declared an ancient monument since the Act came into force. This decision from Whitehall led to an immediate grant of £150,000 to the Mary Rose Trust, and the Environment Secretary, Mr. Michael Heseltine, said that it would be open to the Trust to apply for a further £50,000 to be paid by March 1983.

Hard on the heels of this announcement, H.R.H. the Prince of Wales, speaking to an audience of company chairmen and leaders of financial institutions, once again stressed the importance of the *Mary Rose* in all her aspects. Across the Atlantic, too, the supporters of the *Mary Rose* were rallying to assist in the lifting and the preservation of the ship. After 17 years of exploration and excavation (which had started with such a humble, but inspired, nucleus of divers working from a small open boat) the *Mary Rose* had become a project of international stature. She had achieved a fame in regions unheard of by King Henry VIII.

When looking at the many things brought up from the *Mary Rose* it is important to try and assess them with the eye of the imagination. The images of the twentieth century must be effaced – a hard requirement in itself – and an attempt made to identify with the men who wore these clothes, used these weapons and implements, ate the meat (whose bones we can see) and spat the plum stones over the side.

If it seems to the modern time-traveller that the life of these sailors, soldiers and archers, must have been almost unbearably hard, it must be remembered that the conditions ashore were no better (indeed, the life of a peasant may have been much worse). The Reverend William Harrison, writing in 1577, recorded how conditions in the household had improved since his father's day, "not among the nobility and gentry only but likewise of the lowest sort in most places of our south country." In the north, of course, things were far more backward – clogs instead of leather shoes for one thing and oats rather than wheat for bread. He goes on to say:

> Our fathers yea and we ourselves have lien full oft upon straw pallets, covered only with a sheet, under coverlets made of dogswain or hop harlots (I use their own terms) and a good round log under their heads instead of a bolster. If it were so that our fathers or the good man of the house had a mattress or flockbed and thereto a sack of chaff to rest his head upon, he thought himself to be as well lodged as the lord of the town [village], that paradventure lay seldom in a bed of down or whole feathers. Pillows were thought meet only for women in childbed. As for servants, if they had any sheet above them, it was well, for seldom had they any under their bodies, to keep them from the pricking straws that ran oft through the canvas of the pallet and razed their hardened hides.

Something else must be remembered about the world that these men inhabited: the total population of England and Wales was no more than four millions at the most. Even the countryman of today might be disconcerted by the great miles of land without villages, with few roads – and those mostly little more than tracks – and with dense forests that, though in the temperate zone, were often almost as impassable as those that we nowadays associate with the Tropics. Four-fifths or more of the population lived in remote country districts, the majority of them tending sheep or cultivating the land. Communications were bad, the age of the coach was far distant, and horse and rider were the only means of transmitting urgent messages. An average provincial town had about 5,000 inhabitants – the country was at the door. Only London already foreshadowed the future of the great city that renders its inhabitants anonymous by swamping their individuality and even London, in Tudor times, is unlikely to have had a population of more than 100,000 inhabitants. In considering the background of the men who served in the *Mary Rose* the words of G. M. Trevelyan O.M. in his *English Social History* are all-important: "We must never forget, in picturing the past and specially the remoter past, the want of comforts and luxuries which we take for granted."

Left: A diver hovers over one
of the wheels found in the
forepart of the sunken ship.

Listening to the reports of the divers who have found the skeletons still at the guns, the archer with his long bow and quiver alongside him, one cannot help but speculate what were the last sensations of the men aboard the *Mary Rose*. (Even those of us who have been sunk in ships during a war – and clearly managed to escape – can have no comprehension of those final moments.) Only the imagination of genius can evoke what appears to be the death of a ship – even though this one did not, in fact, sink.

> She gave another lurch to leeward; the lower deadeyes dipped heavily; the mens' feet flew from under them, and they hung kicking above the slanting poop. They could see the ship putting her side in the water, and shouted all together: "She's going!" Forward the forecastle doors flew open, and the watch below were seen leaping out one after another, throwing their arms up; and, falling on hands and knees, scrambled aft on all fours along the high side of the deck, sloping more than the roof of a house. From leeward the seas rose, pursuing them; they looked wretched in a hopeless struggle, like vermin fleeing before a flood; they fought up the weather ladder of the poop one after another, half naked and staring wildly; and as soon as they got up they shot to leeward in clusters, with closed eyes . . .*

Yes, it was probably like that.

It is the greatest of pities that we know nothing of the survivors: archers and men-at-arms most probably, who will have been on the upperdeck when she heeled over and sank. The tale must have been round Portsmouth within an hour of their being rescued by the small boats that one can see pulling out to the wreck. But there were no journalists about in these days, and although the accounts of the sinking, as told by illiterate men, must have been all round the Portsmouth alehouses by the evening, no records at all survive. Everywhere one turns in connection with the sinking of the *Mary Rose* one is met by a question mark – or by silence.

For over four hundred years the deeper silence of the sea engulfed her. It is only now, in the latter part of the twentieth century, that the probing beams of science have rediscovered her, and the ingenuity of man has caused a Tudor world to flower again.

*Joseph Conrad: *The Nigger of the "Narcissus"*.

Left: Two views of the Trust's recovery vessel Sleipner at anchor on the site of the Mary Rose excavations. Twenty years ago the Sleipner helped to raise another famous wreck, the Swedish 17th century warship the Wasa.

Opposite: Spacers from the Mary Rose have provided the answer to a previous puzzle. They were leather discs, pierced with holes for holding arrows so that their delicate flight feathers were not damaged by jostling together. Also in the picture: a leather sword scabbard with knife sheath built into it and an arm-bracer to protect the archer's wrist.

Overleaf: An artist's impression of the Mary Rose. This is based on the illustration of her in the Antony Roll and on contemporary historical evidence.

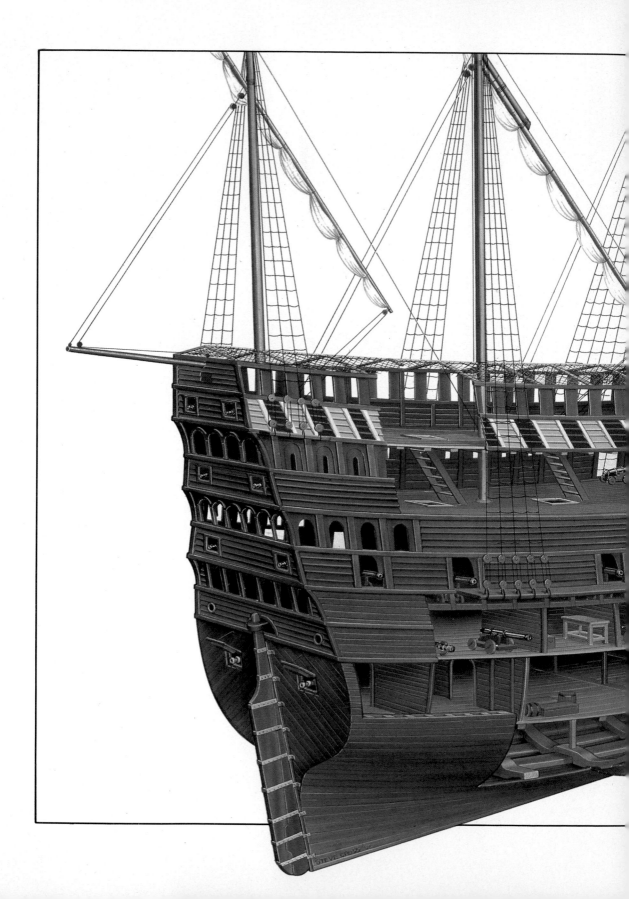

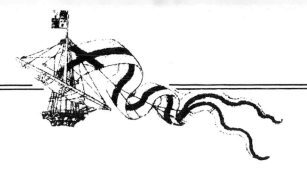

20. *Raising & Preserving the Hull*

IT HAD BEEN Alexander McKee's dream from the very beginning that the hull of the *Mary Rose* should come up, and not just the artefacts inside her. This view had been reciprocated by the other members of the team. From the launching of the Trust, it had been the declared intention to provide a unique showcase for her. Since all the objects from cannon to buckets had been accurately plotted as to their position, with allowance made for the tilt of the ship as she crashed downward on her starboard side and the subsequent carrying away of gear, tackle and cannon, it would be possible to show against the half hull exactly where things were sited in relation to the objects displayed in the intended museum. The hull of the *Mary Rose* would act, in fact, exactly like a giant "cut-out" – with the great difference that it would be real.

The original hope and plan had been to raise the ship in 1981. But, as has been seen, a number of factors had militated against this: there was the necessity to bring up as many articles as possible from the sediment that filled her (at a time when plenty of divers were available) and there was the extra work that was entailed by the necessity to dismantle so much of her decks and other structure. It could be argued that, even though she was not an entire ship, it might have been better – as in the case of the *Wasa* – to excavate down the outboard sides of the ship, pass the strops around her,

Opposite: Colonel Wendell Lewis, Director of Recovery, holds a model reconstruction of the remains of the Mary Rose.

193

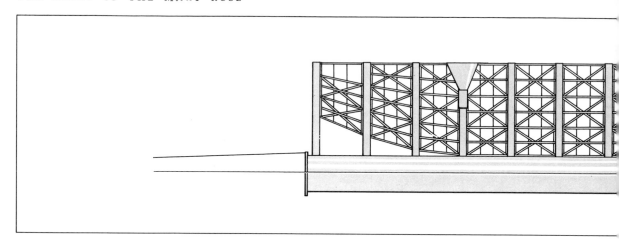

and attend to the lifting process while the artefacts and the containing silt were still inside her. These could have later been sorted out after the half hull had been brought ashore.

But the great drawback has always remained that the *Mary Rose* is not a complete ship: many anchors and trawls have dragged across her over the centuries; her port side is gone; her bow and after castles are collapsed ruins, bearing no relationship to the main body of the hull. There was every likelihood that she might fall to pieces unless special strengthening struts were built into her to sustain what remained of her hull.

In a report completed in January 1982 it was again specifically stated that:

The ship and its contents be recovered, following complete excavation and recording, to form the major constituent of a Tudor Ship Museum in Portsmouth: it being understood that during the period of excavation, recovery and conservation, there will need to be built in opportunities to review and if necessary amend the overall objective.

Prime causes for concern about the state of the remainder of the hull of the *Mary Rose* were the shock waves caused by the crash of the hull on the seabed and the impact of heavy objects falling against the starboard side of the hull, displacing internal structures such as cabin panelling, bulkhead battens and stanchions. The effects of damage from anchors in past years as well as trawls passing over the hull have already been referred to; so too has the mechanical erosion caused by tides and currents. But even more serious, as has been pointed out, are the dangers from biological degradation and, in particular, ship worm. Both gribble and teredo love oak – and the winter of 1981–2 was the last that the *Mary Rose*'s hull would be likely to be able to endure.

194

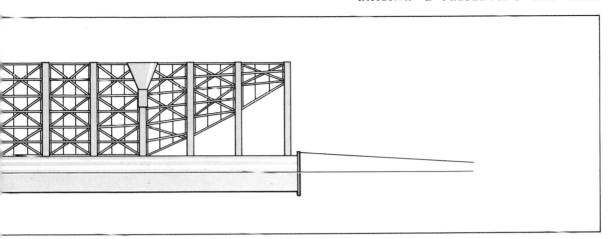

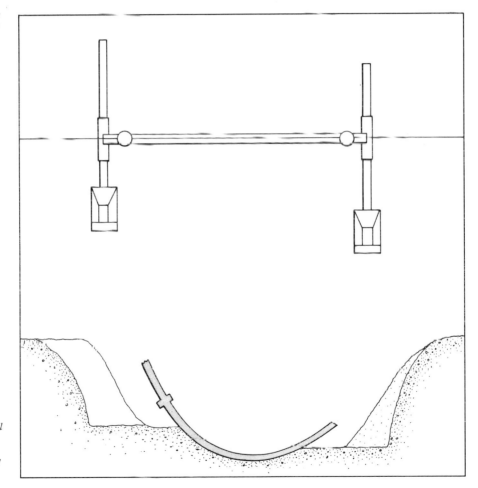

How the Mary Rose *might be raised. These projections date from early 1982. Many modifications will be made before the final plan is established and put into operation.*

A tubular lifting frame with legs will be towed out to the Sliepner *and, using the derrick, the legs will be lowered (right) and the feet fitted and pinned on either side of the hull. The tubes will be flooded.*
Meanwhile, a cradle (above) will be assembled on the quay or slipway and towed out.

195

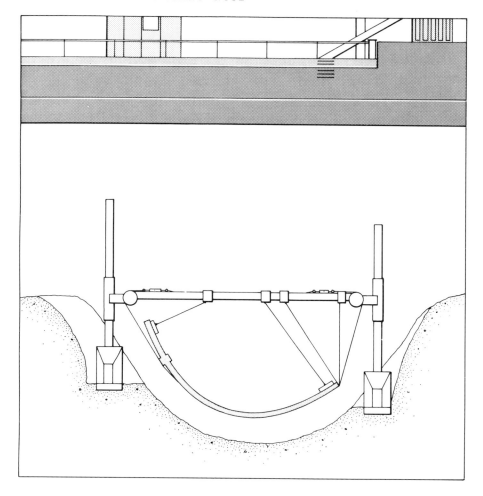

It was concluded that:

The development of the Mary Rose Tudor Ship Museum in the light of the current situation of the Phase One permanent building at Eastney, the offer of a dry dock as a temporary location for the hull in the Dockyard, an alternative proposal for housing the hull in an "off the shelf" building at Eastney, and proposals being developed by the investment bankers, M. J. H. Nightingale and Company, of the possible funding of the museum by means of an issue of securities.

Although about £2 million had been raised by the end of 1981, it was clear that to raise the hull and provide adequate storage for it, as well as to start the immediate conservation of the wooden structure when it came ashore into the hostile air, would certainly require at least a further £2 million. Towards

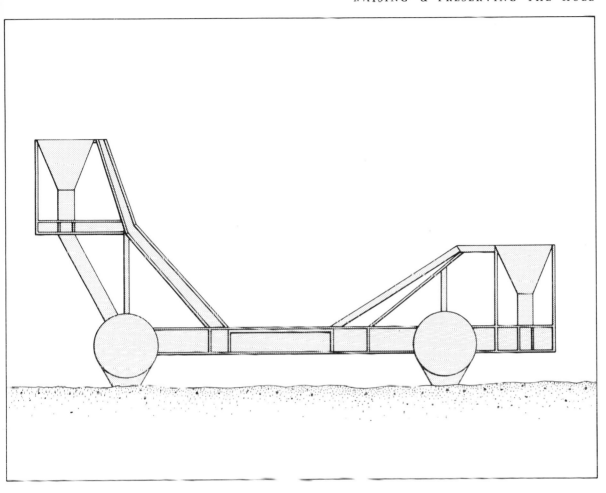

Tunnels will be excavated under the hull (left). Then straps will be passed beneath the hull, around the longitudinal tubes and to the rigging screws on top of the tubes.
Meanwhile, the cradle (above) will be lowered on to the sea bed and its tubes flooded.

the close of 1981 Dr Armand Hammer, the American oil magnate and philanthropist, gave a donation of £50,000 to the Trust conditional on the Trust being able to raise a further £100,000 by the end of the year, which was achieved. The list of benefactors to the Mary Rose Trust in itself reads like a roll-call of British industry. Not only have large sums of money been subscribed to the Trust, but extremely valuable gifts of highly technical and specialized equipment, which have helped towards the work of conservation and preservation to no mean degree.

Interest and enthusiasm from all quarters have revealed, in a Britain whose Navy no longer rules the waves, an interest in our maritime past that might prove startling to politicians – but not to those who are in closer contact with the feeling of the people. In the latest in a long line of bequests to the Trust the National Heritage Memorial Fund in February 1982 pledged £100,000, bringing the total contributions from the Fund to £350,000. Established in 1980 to protect items and buildings of outstanding importance, The National Heritage Memorial Fund thus acknowledged that this wrecked vessel, forgotten for so many centuries, constituted an important memory to the nation of its great history. Perhaps the image of Bluff King Hal, as immortalized by Holbein, did something towards making the *Mary Rose* a symbol of a vanished greatness, which millions regretted but were unable to obviate.

Final conclusions, after many tentative theories had been aired over many months, were that:

The hull must be cradled in such a way that it is neither compressed nor allowed to collapse outwards when lifted into air . . . There have been lengthy discussions with members of the Recovery Panel about designing a comfortable "mattress" to accommodate protruding structures, e.g. wales, chain plates, standards etc., but so far there has been no suggestion made which totally satisfies the requirements of ease of handling underwater, a calculated degree of compression, and ease of removal in sections after the ship is in the workshop ashore. It is vitally important that this problem is solved, and that the matter of support for the hull in air during the museum "work shop" phase is given due consideration.

As much as 300 tons of the original 700 tons (approximately) of the *Mary Rose* will, it is hoped, be raised in the autumn of 1982: even so, with remains of the silts inside her, it will be a formidable task. "It is my view," writes one of the members of the Trust, "that the public will possibly be disappointed when the *Mary Rose* first comes ashore and a new look at the needs of display and interpretation during the first two years is urgently required. We will have much less than half a ship and for the first two years she will only be accessible in workshop conditions and in an environment which will be an effective visitor deterrent . . .

"During the early 1960s when the *Wasa* was sprayed at frequent intervals it was noticeable that most visitors left the galleries during the spraying process, but at *Wasa Varvet* there was an excellent program of films and interpretative displays to keep the visitor amused while the spraying continued."

Something similar will have to be designed around the *Mary Rose*, for it is inconceivable that the ordinary twentieth-century visitor – often with no knowledge of history, nor of the sea and ships – will be able to comprehend this strange Tudor coelacanth which has come up from the depths. Not many people are gifted with imagination, and to invest half a dark-oak Tudor hull with trumpets and pennons and men-at-arms and glinting guns and muscled

The hull will be raised from the sea bed with slings attached to the lifting frame. Stabbing guides will be left on the sea bed so that the Mary Rose *in its lifting frame can be returned there, if things go badly wrong.*

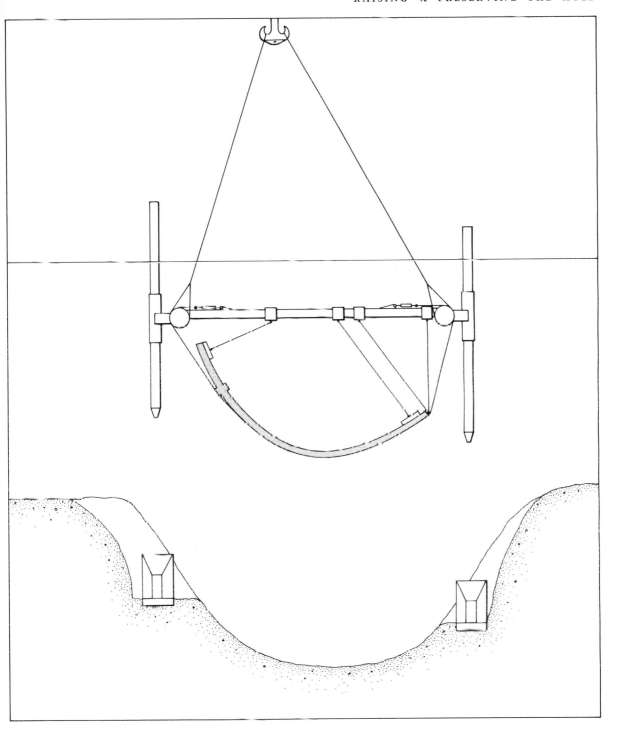

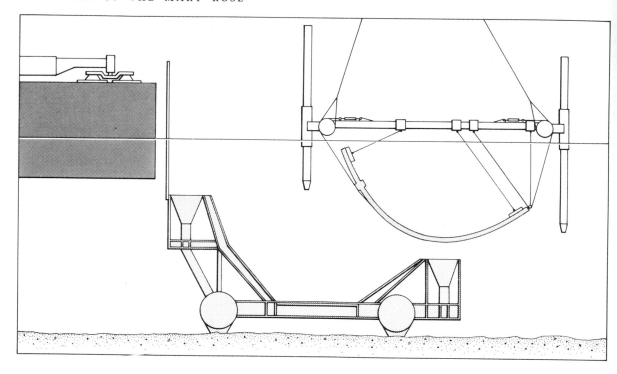

archers is asking a lot of minds that have been softened by the predigested images presented on television.

There are several salvage companies in the world, but there are few men – or none at all – who have had any experience of raising a sixteenth-century warship. "By early 1982," writes the *Tudor News*, "most of the ship's internal timbers will have been removed, leaving just the massive oaken half-hull to be raised in steel framework, in the late summer."

Raising *Mary Rose* will involve strengthening the hull and then tunnelling under it. Through the tunnels will be passed wide nylon lifting straps.

Then it will be possible to lift *Mary Rose* out of her seabed grave with the ship suspended in a stretcher of nylon straps beneath a 150 ft steel lifting frame. The hull can then be transferred into a 159 ft steel cradle to match exactly the profiles of the hull – and the angle at which *Mary Rose* has lain on the seabed for more than four centuries.

Once the hull is encased in the box framework of the lifting frame and cradle, the whole assembly can be lifted to the surface and towed to the shore. . . . So the Mary Rose Trust has assembled a team of diving, engineering, and salvage experts . . . In overall charge will be Col. Wendell Lewis, a retired gunner from Tunbridge Wells, Kent, with wide ex-

The Mary Rose *in its lifting frame will be lifted high enough to give it clearance over the cradle (above). The crane will be boomed up to bring the lifting frame over the cradle. The legs of the lifting frame will be aligned with stabbing guides on either side of the cradle. Finally, slings attached to the cradle will be brought up to the crane hook. The* Mary Rose *and the lifting frame will be lifted through the surface at a speed which will allow water to drain out of all the flooded tubes and give time for the hosing down and pumping out of the hull. Transport (right) will be winched into place and the whole assemblage lowered on to it.*

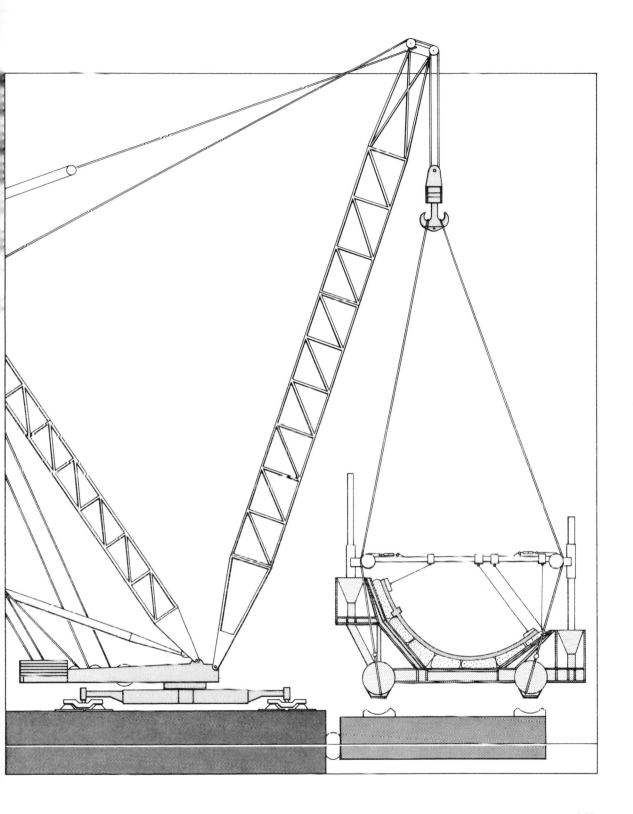

perience of project management, especially in structural engineering. The salvage expertise will be provided by Lt.-Com. Joe Evans, formerly the Royal Navy chief salvage officer, who has in the past tackled tasks such as helping to clear the Suez Canal. The second soldier is a serving officer – Capt. John Brannan, of the Royal Engineers diving establishment at Marchwood. Army divers are likely to play an important supporting role in carrying out the engineering diving involved in recovery.

Engineers, designers, equipment specialists and quantity surveyors complete the membership of the team . . . Until the final stages of the project, *Mary Rose* will remain something of an enigma.

Bringing the hull ashore will be a difficult task in itself, but the conservation of these old timbers, once exposed to the air, will be yet another thing. Fortunately, the team have available to them not only the hard-won expertise of those who worked (and are still working) on the *Wasa*, but of the Dutch who have brought up wooden ships recovered during the reclamation of land from the sea. The *Mary Rose* diving team will play a major part throughout. It is strange, perhaps, that man should now go under the sea to try and bring back that which was built out of earthly materials upon the land, and to try and reconstitute them as a memorial to his ancestors. But, then, men are now leaving the planet Earth with an ultimate view to the colonization of the heavens. The exploration of inner space – the sea itself – remains one of the greatest challenges left to that ever-inquisitive mammal, man.

The Mary Rose Trust, 1982

Acknowledgements

The Trust is indebted not only to the staff but also the many volunteers, both divers and others, without whom the project could not have been managed.

The Trust is deeply grateful for the generosity of many donors, both public and private, and supporters too numerous to name.

The publisher would like to thank the Mary Rose Trust who supplied all the illustrations in the book except for the following:

Reproduced by Gracious Permission of Her Majesty the Queen, pages 16–17

Reproduced by permission of the Master and Fellows of Magdalene College, Cambridge, pages 14–15, 16, 28–29, 30–31, 34, 50–51, 53, 57, 58–59

Crown Copyright, Science Museum London, pages 18, 20–21, 24

Photo, Science Museum London, pages 19, 26, 27, 46–47, 49

Photographs by Adam Woolfitt by kind permission of *Reader's Digest*, pages 122, 123, 124, 189

Portsmouth City Museums, pages 10, 11, 12, 13, 22, 24, 32, 33, 40, 41, 42, 43, 67, 75, 76, 78, 79, 89 and colour page 87

Portsmouth and Sunderland Newspapers Ltd, pages 43, 44, 77, 81, 82, 84, 95, 123, 146, 168

The British Library, page 57

The National Maritime Museum, London, pages 68–69

The National Portrait Gallery, page 49

The Daily Telegraph, page 41, and colour page 121

Library of the Ministère de la Guerre, Paris, pages 24, 34, 55, 65, 82, 94, 100, 107, 143, 150, 181

Photographs International Ltd, page 88.

The line illustrations on pages 55, 61, 116, 119, 120, 142, 143, 147, 148, 149 are © Shirley Willis, 1982

The colour cut-away illustration of Mary Rose and illustrations on pages 194, 195, 196, 197, 199, 200, 201 are © Steven Cross, 1982

The publishers would like to thank members of the Mary Rose Trust for their help in producing this book.

Index